D1502790

It Can't Be That Bad
The Stories of My Police Career

To the Albert Family,
My "Eagles" friends.
I wish you good health
and happiness in your new
home. I hope you like my
book.   Take care,

This book is dedicated to
Karen Bizzell
my wife who was with me through it all
and allowed me to follow my dreams
and to my beautiful daughter
Jordyn Bizzell
my greatest achievement

Table of Contents

Introduction

Chapter 1

Chapter 2

Chapter 3

Chapter 4

Chapter 5

Chapter 6

Chapter 7

Chapter 8

Chapter 9

Chapter 10

Chapter 11

Chapter 12

Chapter 13

Chapter 14

Chapter 15

Chapter 16

Chapter 17

Chapter 18

Chapter 19

Chapter 20

Chapter 21

Chapter 22

Chapter 23

Chapter 24

Chapter 25

Chapter 26

Chapter 27

Chapter 28

Chapter 29

Conclusion

Every police officer can tell you some stories. I used to always say officers should definitely write down the good ones, because there are too many to remember without help. The average police officer will see a great deal and handle a great deal of tragedy during their career. Police officers end up dealing with problems that nobody else, including the caller, wants to address.

My story will walk you along the path I chose in life of becoming a police officer and show you my career through many stories that have never been told. I will tell of the challenges of becoming a police officer, the challenges on the job, and the biggest challenge of having to leave the force after becoming disabled.

My story could have played out anywhere. I know that stories like these are playing out in many inner-city police departments in America and officers are doing heroic deeds every single day they are on the job, whether in response to calls, in attempts to protect others, or to affect the arrest of violent suspects. I have chosen to tell my police stories without revealing the names of the individuals involved or even mentioning the city where it all occurred. With little effort, someone could identify the city where I served as an officer or research and identify everyone involved, but that isn't the point of the story.

The stories document the dangers of policing and will tell of the many injuries that I sustained on the job. There were five separate incidents which led to injuries that required orthopedic surgeries for me to recover. The stories also include the head injuries sustained while working and my ultimate diagnosis of Parkinson's disease, which resulted in my leaving the police department.

During my career, I heard countless critiques of police officer's work, their response to something, or their actions taken. The newspapers, television reporters, civil rights groups, neighborhood groups, and even your average citizen can be quick to tell what an officer should have done. Everyone outside of policing have great ideas about how the job should be accomplished and are certainly quick to comment when the job isn't done up to their standard.

This is America and when we are talking about policing the streets, it can't be that bad.

Chapter 1

For as long as I can remember, I always envisioned myself being a police officer. I believe that it is true that some people have desires in their DNA or in their genetic make-up. I am not certain where my knowledge of policing came from and perhaps I really didn't know exactly what officers did on a daily basis prior to making that career decision. I grew up before "Cops" was filmed on location and before those suspects were assumed innocent in a court of law. However, the first time I watched the show it was easy to see that the suspects were guilty. My desire to become an officer was rooted in the basic principle of right and wrong and to protect those that are victimized by others. Even as a child, I never liked to see anyone being taken advantage of or victimized. I have always been a peacemaker, and I am sure there is a psychiatrist somewhere that will tell you it's because I am the middle child.

I am not sure who should get the original credit for the theory of three types of people in the world – sheep, wolves, and sheepdogs. I know that Dave Grossmann, the author of On Killing talks about it in lectures and in his books, but states it is not his theory. The theory can be explained something like this. A "sheep" person is anyone in the world who goes about their daily lives with no intention of hurting any other person or ever exhibiting violence. A "wolf" person is a person who feeds off of the sheep, whether it is through committing physical violence or property crimes toward the sheep. A "sheepdog" person is courageous enough to face the violence to protect the sheep from the wolves. The sheepdog lives to confront the wolves and track them down to end their reign of terror over the sheep. I have lived my life as a sheepdog.

I knew that I always wanted to work in law enforcement. When I was growing up, I just assumed that I would be a police officer. After high school, I started college at a community college with a Criminal Justice major. I attended the community college for a year and transferred to the local university. So many people told me I should do "something more" with my life, whatever that means. I am not sure if I could even count a handful of people that actually supported my idea of becoming a police officer.

I decided to work toward a position in federal law enforcement, and had set my sights on the FBI. After researching the FBI, I came to the conclusion that they hired many attorneys and CPA's, so I changed my major at the university to Accounting. Society really doesn't like attorneys. Even today, when I think of attorneys I am reminded of an old joke (and there are plenty). A terrible tragedy happened today. A bus full of attorneys was traveling down a mountainside after a big convention. The driver lost control, went through the guardrail, and everyone on the bus perished. The tragedy was that there was one empty seat.

I continued to pursue the position of a Special Agent in the FBI. I graduated from the university's business school as their very first student ever to have a dual major of a BSBA in Accountancy and Finance and thanks to rounding up I had a 3.5 GPA. Unfortunately for me it was 1993. I was advised by the FBI recruiter that they may only hire a couple special agents throughout the entire country that year and that they prefer candidates to have at least five years of experience in their "field of expertise". I was born 20 years too late for the FBI hiring spree in the mid 1970's. I also still needed to pass the national CPA exam and work in a public accounting firm for one year to even obtain my CPA license.

I was able to pass the CPA exam and I worked in a small public CPA firm for two years. I became Michael D. Bizzell, CPA and I worked at a desk in a tiny office for an average of 50 plus hours a week. My wife worked evening shift as a registered nurse. To blow off stress after work I would run two miles to the local gym, lift weights, and then run back home. I was miserable.

We moved to Florida in April of 1996. I obtained a position with another small public CPA firm and continued working long weeks. I had contacted the police department and was advised that they really were not hiring and they preferred applicants that were already certified in law enforcement by the State of Florida. I learned about the police academy and started the long process for applying and completing the background check. Even to get into the academy the background check is pretty thorough. You consent to a criminal history check, running your fingerprints through the FBI database, they verify every residence, school, place of employment, talk to your neighbors, and check with your third grade teacher that you were socially adjusted. That last requirement may be an exaggeration.

I had asked the academy to not contact the CPA firm where I was working at until the last step in the approval process, but that request was overlooked. The CPA partners in the firm where I worked were not pleased when the academy mailed the background verification to them. I was able to stay on the CPA treadmill, but decided I should find another job. I knew that it is always an easier process to find a new job while still employed. I also knew that nothing was happening quickly with hiring at the police department, and the police academy was only running a couple of classes per year.

I obtained a new position in the corporate headquarters of a large regional drug store. I was going

3

to be a "Regional Analyst" in the inventory accounting department. I was assigned all of the stores in the regions of Texas, Mid-South, and Mid-Atlantic, which included about 1,250 individual stores and 1,250 of anything is a great deal to keep track of. Some of my responsibilities were to travel to the regional offices and teach the regional managers how the corporate office completes the financial accounting for individual store inventories. Yes, the new employee was sent out to teach regional managers, with 20 plus years of company experience, how things worked. I was also eventually tasked with compiling a weekly summary of the entire corporation's operations every Monday morning. The corporate CEO and Board of Directors used my report in their weekly Director's meeting to make the decisions for the entire corporation. I was not too impressed with how big corporate accounting offices operated; I was just the new guy, right? The trips on the small corporate jet were fun, but the new position required 60 plus hours a week and, yes, I was still miserable.

Chapter 2

I had been married for five years and was living in Florida, in a city where my wife and I planned to live our lives together. I guess the biggest draw for us was the weather, but I had some friends and family in the area also. I was still figuring out all of the required steps to obtain a position as a police officer and how to expedite that process. I discovered in Florida there are specific college courses that a candidate must take before he can sit for the State of Florida Law Enforcement Certification test. There are two ways you can earn the credit for these courses which are taking the courses while working toward a college degree or through a full time police academy. At the time almost every police agency was also requiring a minimum of 60 college credits even to complete an application. I chose to attend the full time police academy, which operated Monday through Friday, 0800 hours to 1700 hours, and lasted 17 weeks. During this time, I was able to cut my corporate accounting position down to only working a full day on Saturday.

I will never forget my first day of the police academy. I had already purchased all of the required supplies, my textbooks, and was wearing the required khaki uniform. I was one of the first, if not, the first student to arrive. The lead instructor was an Officer D, who was an active and sworn law enforcement officer from the agency that I had hoped to work for. The class started at 0800 hours and Officer D was introducing himself and explaining the rules to the class. About ten minutes into his presentation the final student decided to show up, so he was welcomed with a barrage of negative comments from Officer D. It was very clear that you wanted to follow all of the rules.

I was 28 years old, which was not the oldest student but older than most and certainly older than the minimum required age of 21. Everybody loves day one of any class. "Please stand by your desk, state your name, and introduce yourselves". I was sitting in the last column of desks to introduce ourselves and everything seemed to be going very smoothly. There were 31 students in my class and all of us seemed to have very different backgrounds. By the time it was my turn Officer D was joking around and trying to get to know the students in a friendly way.

I stood up next to my desk and stated, "Hello, my name is Mike Bizzell". Officer D quickly interrupted me, "Now wait a minute! Don't stand there with your hands in your pockets". Officer D continued with what seemed like a ten minute lecture on officer safety and how your hands must always be ready to react. No one else had received the pleasure of generating a class lecture but me. I continued standing for the entire time of his lecturing the class and this became my first lesson in policing. I had already scheduled an obstacle course for the following day at the police department as part of the hiring process, so at the end of my first day, I had to ask Officer D if I could come in late the next day to the academy. I think I really made a great first impression.

The academy was broken up into sections, which were law, interpersonal skills, patrol, communications, firearms, driving, and self-defense. The sections were taught by assistant state attorneys, defense attorneys, retired and active police officers, and a couple of college professors. Eventually, I made pretty good friends with Officer D and I would have to say that I enjoyed my time at the academy. I remember one teaching officer, Officer R, stating to a small group of us as we bantered in the hall, "You all are enjoying re-telling the funny stories of your time in the academy, just wait until you are out on the street and the stories are real". There ended up being a lot of truth to that statement.

Based on our prior experience, Officer D assigned a class leader and a "Sergeant at Arms" to two other students. The positions were mostly symbolic, but were needed in case some problems arose. I have always been a silent leader. I am the guy that helps others out behind the scenes and really never looking to receive credit for it. However, my actions in the academy were noticed by a group of my fellow students and at the end of the academy they purchased a gift of a rock paper weight for me that stated, "Real leaders are ordinary people with extraordinary determination". I was touched by their thoughtfulness and I still have that paper weight today, staring at me as I type my story.

Two weeks prior to graduating from the academy, I was hired by the agency where I wanted to work. Since I was hired, I was able to graduate in a police uniform along with three other recruits of the class already hired by the city. In truth we were not sworn officers, because we still needed to take a state certification exam to prove that we actually learned something in the academy. After graduation and taking the exam, the four of us were in limbo until we received our test scores from the State of Florida. For approximately two weeks, the four of us kind of hung out in the police training building doing odd tasks for anyone in the police training division. My specialty became carrying empty cardboard boxes to the dumpster at the end of the day. We all passed the state exam, so the next step was to become "sworn" law enforcement officers in front of a civil court judge. Our swearing in ceremony was pretty uneventful, since our group of four was so small. We basically showed up at the courtroom and the judge had us swear to the law enforcement oath in between two of the cases on his docket.

The State of Florida Oath is as follows: I <u>Michael Bizzell</u>, do solemnly swear to discharge all of the duties incumbent upon me as a police officer of the City, in the State of Florida, to the best of my ability, without favor or affection, and in doing so to uphold and support the

7

Law Enforcement Code of Ethics of my profession, so help me God. (Yes, the state of Florida mentions God, so please don't tell the atheists).

The next step in the training was the Field Training Unit with the city. This unit is exactly what you think it is, police training out in the field or on the street. The field training is broken up into "phases" one through four. Each phase is supposed to move more of the responsibility from the field training officer to the probationary officer. Every officer is hired on probation for the first year, so the department can determine if they meet acceptable standards. Probationary officers can be "fired" or let go at any time during their first year, if they are "not responding to training". The average "washout" rate for recruits from day one of the academy through the end of an officer's first year is almost 50%. The city was broken up into three districts, so they attempt to assign a new district for each phase to enable each trainee the chance to geographically learn the entire city. It is kind of a roll of the dice as to which shift you ended up working, because you simply worked the shift that your field training officer was assigned.

In almost any professional career, there is a transition phase of taking what you have learned in the classroom and applying it to your job in the field. In policing there are many checklists that you must either mentally or physically check off prior to "hitting the street". The first checklist is getting dressed. Every officer in uniform should be professional and present that image to the community. All uniformed officers should be that, uniform, or simply meaning dressed the same. There are minor differences on where a particular officer wants to keep his equipment on their duty belt, but basically officers carry the same equipment on their uniform. The next checklist is all of the extra required equipment carried in the police cruiser, such as rain gear, riot gear, trauma kits, CPR masks, property bags, evidence bags, etc. Every officer at the time also carried a file box of forms because there is a tremendous amount of paperwork generated by police officers. Every interaction that an officer has on a call with a citizen must be documented in some way. Depending on the type of call that you are dispatched to there are different forms that must be filled out or a different report that must be typed and submitted. My typing class in high school helped me in college, but it really paid off in my police career. Finally, since you don't own the cruiser, it needs to be checked inside and out for damage, prior officer's property, or prior suspect's weapons or evidence in the rear seat compartment for your own safety.

Those procedures kind of sound like a full day's work but now you are finally ready to hit the street. The uniformed patrol officers of any police department are the "911 responders" of the department. Patrol officers are directed by the communications center to respond to calls that come in either through the 911 center or directly to communications. When patrol officers are not working a dispatched call, they are either finishing paperwork or conducting self-initiated activity. Patrol officers that have policing in their DNA create plenty of self-initiated activity. Every officer on the street eventually creates his own police personality by how he works and how he interacts with not only other officers, but every individual on the street. Officers eventually throughout their career will tend to gravitate toward an area in policing that they enjoy, but initially everyone starts out in patrol.

Finally, after 28 years, I am sitting in the driver's seat of a marked police cruiser, in full uniform, and hitting the street with my field training officer (FTO) partner. What the hell am I supposed to do now?

Chapter 3

There were definitely shorter paths I could have traveled to land in the driver's seat of the marked cruiser in the police field training division. However, it's hard to put a value on education and work experience. Besides, if I screwed up I could always go back to working in accounting. Ha!

For my phase one of training, I was assigned to District One, dayshift, and my field training officer was Officer M, who had approximately 18 years on the department. Officer M had just joined the Field Training Unit, so I was actually his first probationary officer. Looking back, I can appreciate that there was a learning curve for both of us, although Officer M was a very seasoned veteran.

One of the first things an officer has to learn is geographic orientation. Obviously, an officer must know the directions north, south, east, and west, but they must also be able to travel from point A to point B in the shortest amount of time. Officers also have to be able to locate the address that the communications center sends them to. For some recruits, it is a big win simply finding their way back to the station at the end of the first day. I knew a few of the main roads in the City because I had lived in Florida for about 2 years, but I really did not know the City. To learn any new city thoroughly you need to start with all the main roads that travel to different parts of the city and eventually you'll learn the neighborhoods. It also helps to remember different landmarks such as, the "Marathon gas station is on the corner of 18th Avenue". Once you are a functioning police officer it is imperative that you know your exact location at every moment. Your life or someone else's may depend on that fact.

Another thing that a new recruit must learn is to listen to the police radio. You basically are given a new name, or call sign, and are expected to respond to it.

My first call sign was 214A or "214 Alpha". It takes a few days to obtain an "ear for the radio". Eventually, you not only hear communications calling you, but you are also aware of everyone else's calls too. An experienced officer can follow the radio activity while completing all of his own tasks, interviews, etc.

During my first week, we were dispatched to the scene of an unattended death. Before I was an officer, I really did not give too much thought about the fact that people die. Sure I had been to funerals of family members and friends, but in this world people die. Many people die every day in every state, in every city, in different neighborhoods, in various accidents, due to various health problems, people grow old, people are murdered, people commit suicide, and they all die wherever they are at the time.

To a rookie police officer every death is a homicide and that's actually how every death should be treated until it is proven otherwise because every life is sacred and should be respected. Ultimately, every death falls under the jurisdiction of the Medical Examiner's Office in Florida. If someone dies while not under the direct care of a doctor, it is the responsibility of the police officer to determine what happened and to ensure that no crime had been committed. The police call the Medical Examiner's Office from the scene of the death with the brief details about the death and the Medical Examiner's Office will make a decision whether they want to pick up the body or they release it to a funeral home. If the deceased was under a doctor's care and the doctor is willing to sign a death certificate, then they usually will release the body. Many times you simply have a dead person with no obvious signs of trauma, so the Medical Examiner will want the body to determine the cause of death. In all cases of homicide or suicide, the body is picked up by the Medical Examiner's Office.

In the majority of cases of "unattended death" the family needs a great deal of guidance through the process and hardly anyone purchases prearranged funerals even if they are a "deal". The loved ones are left behind to make decisions on what funeral home they will contact and how to notify other loved ones about the death. Some scenes are peaceful and orderly, some are screaming chaotic messes, some are lonely, and some are weeks old with smells that never go away.

A police officer's job is not complete until he ensures that there is not any trauma to the body or any known cause of death. This process includes removing clothing of the deceased to view every square inch of the deceased's body. The last thing you would want to happen would be to send a body to the Medical Examiner with an unknown bullet hole, stab wound, needle marks, etc. This process and time to complete that task can be a little unsettling for a family. It can be awkward to know someone is going to check under your family member's clothing, so I always tried to explain it well and completed the task in private. Death is not usually pretty and it certainly doesn't smell good no matter how "fresh" death occurred. However, there usually is a great sense of peacefulness of the deceased.

***

The communications center dispatcher had advised that the call came through "911" from the deceased's wife, rescue units were already on scene, and had pronounced the death. Upon arrival, I spoke briefly with rescue units, obtained their information, and the details of their actions. Next, I spoke to the deceased's wife, Mrs. T., who was a 60 year old black female. Mrs. T. advised that at approximately 0530 hours her husband awoke and climbed out of bed as he does most mornings. Mrs. T. advised that her husband would complain of headaches, but did not have any known health problems. Mrs. T. advised that she awoke and

13

found her husband in his recliner and he appeared to be deceased. Mrs. T. initially called her sister-in-law, who told her to call "911" right away. It is very common that people do not know what to do or who to call and Mrs. T. had just found out that she was a widow and the love of her life was gone.

Mr. T. appeared to have been resting in his recliner with his hands folded, almost in prayer, and probably passed away in his sleep. I contacted his doctor's office through the V.A. hospital and they would not sign a death certificate, so the Medical Examiner's Office would take custody of the body. I completed all of my responsibilities, Mr. T. was picked up, and I left Mrs. T. in the care of other family members. We were dispatched to the call at 1045 hours and left the residence at 1315 hours. I came into Mrs. T's life for just two and a half hours and removed her husband forever. This is one example of why I always say police get to meet people on the worst day of their lives. Mrs. T., however, was a very kind and gracious woman and wrote a "good guy" letter to the chief thanking me for my services. I never saw her again.

***

Not very long after the first death call, I was dispatched to another "unattended death", which was a stark contrast to the first call. The call initially came in to dispatch as a "check welfare" call on a son who had not been in contact with his mother for a few weeks. The mother wanted officers to respond to the residence and verify that her son was alright. Upon arrival, officers found no answer at the unlocked door, entered, and located the subject deceased inside. A few minutes later I was dispatched to handle the call, because I was the "rookie" in training.

The deceased had been living inside an old residence that you would assume was abandoned. Over half of the windows were boarded up and everything about the house was in disrepair. There was almost no furniture inside and the few pieces that were there looked like they had come from the garbage dump. Nothing inside the home had been cleaned in decades and it clearly was not fit for human habitation. At approximately twenty feet from the front door, you could start to smell the odor from the deceased. The deceased was a 40 year old black male, who was a heroin addict. The deceased was located in a tiny bathroom in the house. The deceased was shooting up with heroin while going to the bathroom when he died and fell off the toilet. The deceased's body almost came apart as we checked it for any sign of trauma. There was no family to console, with this death scene.

***

While still in training, I was dispatched to another death call, but this time it was called in as a suicide. Upon arrival, I observed a 27 year old white female who had hung herself. The female was lesbian and had a bad argument with her girlfriend. After the argument the girlfriend went for a short walk and came back home to find the deceased hanging by her neck. The deceased had written a quick, short suicide note addressing the argument and mentioning her parents being ashamed of her. The deceased had then tied an extension cord around her neck, made a small loop in the middle, and then hooked it onto a hanging hook that had been screwed into the frame of a doorway. Normally the hanging hook would be used to hold a plant or something decorative and would break or pull out with too much weight. On that day, the hanging hook held strong enough to hold a 140 pound female for at least twenty minutes.

The maintenance man at the apartment unhooked the deceased prior to my arrival after he had heard the screams from the girlfriend. Although the cord had been loosened from the neck, the deceased's entire head was purple above the line in her neck and it stayed that way. This was a sad situation for both the deceased and for all the living that cared for her. The young girl chose a permanent solution for all of her temporary problems and left behind many individuals that I am certain never fully recovered from her death.

***

Now all calls in my training were obviously not death calls. Detective Q called over the radio that he was just involved in an accident and that another driver had hit him from behind. The communications center dispatched me to respond and handle the accident call. Upon arrival, I observe Detective Q standing in a nearby parking lot talking with a 20 year old black male. Detective Q advised that the black male was the driver in the other vehicle and that the black male had a suspended driver's license. I placed the black male suspect under arrest by handcuffing him, searching him, and putting him into the rear of my cruiser. Detective Q issued the suspect a criminal traffic citation with a notice to appear at a specific court date. We moved the suspect's vehicle to a nearby parking lot and the suspect was released at the scene. At that moment, it seemed like everything went well on the call.

A few hours later, I arrested a juvenile for something and took him out to the juvenile jail facility. Prior to leaving the facility, I checked my rear seat for any contraband that could have been left by the juvenile and located a clear baggie of crack cocaine. I went back inside the facility with my FTO and we started to interrogate the juvenile about the crack cocaine. The juvenile was adamant that the cocaine was not his, not that this was a surprise, but I actually believed him. I thought back on my day and realized that I had not cleared the rear seat after arresting the black male for the suspended license. I had to tuck my tail between my legs and tell my FTO my mistake. We had to put the

16

narcotics in for destruction and I never made that mistake again for the rest of my career.

***

In my third month of training, I was working the midnight shift. On one call, I was dispatched to a domestic battery, which is a call that every officer becomes very familiar with. It was approximately 0200 hours, but domestic calls happen round the clock. The fire rescue units were also dispatched, due to the fact that the female victim was pregnant. Upon arrival, I discovered that the victim could only speak Spanish and there were no Spanish speaking officers working at that time. I had to call the AT&T language line and coordinate an interview with the victim. The victim's husband had physically battered his pregnant wife and left her with minimal injuries. Since he knew or should have known that she was pregnant, the battery offense was a felony in the State of Florida. The family had two children and of course alcohol was a factor for the husband's actions. This domestic call really wasn't any different than the couple thousand other domestics that would follow in my career. However, it always stuck out in my mind, because I returned two nights later anonymously leaving a bag of clothing on the porch for the female that included some maternity clothing. Genuine gifts are things that are given freely where a maximum of two people know about the gift, you and the person who receives it.

***

The remainder of my time in the field training unit went pretty well. I had made it to Phase four, which is the final phase. During this phase, the trainee is supposed to function on their own with the FTO in plainclothes evaluating them. I was back on dayshift and my FTO partner had me sneak to the station, so he could take care of some business. I was dispatched to an in progress shots fired at a business, with a great

17

description of a black male suspect that left on a bike. The station was really not that far out of my area, but I knew I would be delayed getting to the cruiser and getting to the scene. Looking back, I could see that for my FTO it was simply another shots fired call, but for me it was the biggest call of the week.

I had the back-up units circulate for the suspect and one of them spotted the suspect cutting through a neighborhood. The suspect was finally stopped by units approximately nine blocks away from the shooting scene prior to my arrival. The shooting occurred at a meat market. Upon arrival to the scene, it appeared like business as usual, as people were coming and going from the store as if nothing had happened. The only witness willing to speak was one of the employees, who had made the call to "911" and he pointed out the fresh bullet holes in the front of the store. I also located a vehicle parked out front with a bullet hole. This was an attempt homicide but there was no "victim" from the offense that was willing to speak to the police. The suspect was charged under the Throwing Deadly Missiles statute, which covers shooting into an occupied structure along with other charges. A couple years later the suspect took a plea deal on a concealed firearm charge for all of the charges and served out the remainder of a five year sentence. It is very true that the wheels of justice turn slowly.

Chapter 4

I was released from the field training unit and sent to patrol as a solo police officer. By this time in my career, I had been an employee of the city for almost five months and I was considered a probationary police officer until I made it through a total of twelve months. I mentioned before that there was an approximate 50% wash out rate from day one of the academy to the end of the first year, so that fact is always on a rookie police officer's mind. I remember looking over at the empty front seat, where my FTOs used to sit and feeling mixed emotions. I was assigned to an evening shift that worked 1600 hours to 2400 hours with rotating days off.

Almost right away, I started working closely with Officer D, who was also a rookie in patrol just a couple months ahead of me. For the next two years, Officer D and I became an inseparable team that worked very aggressively together against criminals. For part of that time, we had a Sergeant S, who retired at the end of my second year. Upon his retirement, Sergeant S pulled myself and Officer D aside and stated, "I wanted to let you both know that in my 25 years of policing, I have never seen two officers with more natural instincts and capabilities as you two, especially you all working together".

***

Everything didn't go perfectly for Officer D and I, but we did make a hell of a crime fighting team. One day we were dispatched to a call of an aggravated assault. The communications center advised that there was a female caller advising that her boyfriend pulled a twelve inch butcher knife on her and threatened to kill her. Upon arrival, a black female came walking out from the residence with her arms crossed on her chest and advised that the boyfriend ran from the house. I stood by as Officer D interviewed her for about five minutes about what happened. Officer D eventually asked her about the knife and the female stated, "yeah this knife", as she uncrossed her arms revealing a twelve inch butcher knife in hand that had been hidden along her tri-cep muscle. Both Officer D and I, had her place the knife down and realized that we had just made a terrible officer safety mistake.

***

On another day, I had my first accident in a police cruiser. Police officers drive many miles, for many hours, and have to drive aggressively, so it is no surprise that they bend a few bumpers. The communications center advised that there was a caller that was following a DUI driver. There were not any officers in the vicinity of the caller and the DUI driver was driving away from my location. I was attempting to respond to the call and catch up to the DUI driver before they reached their destination. I reached a point in the roadway where there were two hard curves in the road. I was traveling too fast as I entered the second curve and went off the roadway striking a sign for the oncoming traffic. There was minimal damage to the cruiser and worse damage to my pride. The funny part about the accident was I had hit a "dangerous curve" sign.

***

Ironically a few months later, Officer D and I responded to a similar call together. We had been parked somewhere talking, when we were both dispatched to a call of a DUI driver with the complainant following behind the DUI driver. I followed behind Officer D as we headed toward the call. Both of us were driving a little fast because we were not close to the driver's location at all. We were headed toward a very sharp rise in the road that was known as "thrill hill". I am sure it obtained its' name because if you go over it faster than 15 mph you can feel it in your stomach. As we approached "thrill hill", I was saying to Officer D in my mind "ok slow down". Officer D never touched his brakes and when his cruiser came off the peak of the hill I could see the entire undercarriage of the vehicle. I was quite certain the cruiser was going to land on the front bumper and flip forward onto the roof. Somehow the vehicle landed on the wheels and, I was able to continue driving while laughing hysterically.

***

There was one boarding house in particular that we made an exceptional number of drug arrests from. Pretty much everyone that went to the house or lived there were involved in narcotics. There were about six units that were one room a piece with a shared kitchen and bathroom. There wasn't a single piece of furniture in the entire building that held any value and nothing had ever been cleaned.

On one particular evening, a small group of officers checked out at the structure. After talking to the "manager" on scene, who was also a crack addict, we knocked on the door to unit number five. The manager had advised that no one was supposed to live in the unit, but someone was inside. Two females opened the door and after a brief conversation one of the females, a citizen of England, was placed under arrest for possession of crack cocaine. The second female was eventually released and instructed not to return to unit number five. I transported the arrested female to jail and returned to the area.

After being back in the area for a few minutes, Officer J stopped a black male on a bike that was one block from the boarding house with a television on the handlebars. Now this occurred in the year of 1999, so the television was an old tube type that was big and bulky. Officer J had me confirm that the television was the same television that was inside room number five, where we had just made the cocaine arrest and it was.

Officer J arrests the suspect for a burglary to unit number five. The assistant state attorney would later tell Officer J that she did not believe that Officer J had reasonable suspicion to stop the arrested and that it was not suspicious to be riding a bike at 2300 hours with a large tube television on the handlebars. This obviously wasn't the crime of the century, but sometimes the state attorney's office looked for reasons to "flush" cases from a system that was overloaded.

***

On another occasion, Officer D, Officer B, and I set up and watched activity at that same boarding house. At the time, Officer B was working as our "acting sergeant", which meant he was our supervisor at the moment. We checked out with the communications center at the location and started working on a different radio channel than other patrol officers in the area. Officer D was in the bushes on the north side of a parking lot watching and Acting Sergeant B was on the south side of the boarding house. The main door that everyone used was on the north side of the building and the parking lot sat to the north of that door. I had started to walk up to the main door, when a car pulled into the parking lot. I crouched down right beside the small porch in front of the main door.

The vehicle pulled right up to the stairs that led up to the porch, the doors opened, and two black males exited the vehicle. The vehicle was still running with the doors open as the two walked up onto the porch. I was able to whisper into my police radio that they were conducting a narcotic transaction with another black male that had come to the door. The subjects were only about ten feet away from me and I have no idea how they did not initially see me hiding in plain sight. I advised for all of us to move in to affect an arrest on the subjects. Officer D started running up from across the parking lot and I jumped up from my hiding spot.

The suspects ran toward their vehicle. I grabbed ahold of the passenger, but his momentum pulled me into the suspect vehicle. My feet were still outside of the vehicle and a portion of my upper body was inside the vehicle. The driver of the suspect vehicle had also made it back inside the car, threw the transmission in reverse, and punched the gas. I was hit extremely hard by the door and the frame of the vehicle. I assume that the suspect realized that he may end up killing me after pulling me along with them for about twenty five feet and he slammed on the brakes. When the vehicle had slowed, I took that opportunity to push away from the vehicle's door cavity and rolled across the parking lot. Officer D had made it in front of the vehicle and had his firearm pointed at the driver. Acting Sergeant B was running up from the south yelling, "Don't shoot, don't shoot", because he knew that the imminent threat of death or great bodily harm to me had passed. The driver of the suspect vehicle had only pushed the brakes briefly and was right back on the accelerator backing out to the street and racing off northbound. From the time we moved to affect the arrests till the suspects were totally out of sight took about five seconds. Shit happens fast!

I stood up and initially attempted to change my radio back to the patrol channel, but the suspects were pretty much gone. We all knew that we were too far from our own police cruisers and we were not going to get a back-up officer quick enough. The three of us stood there in the parking lot and had a little pow-wow while I dusted myself off. Acting Sergeant B started out by saying, "Well I think we pretty much fucked that whole thing up from the start" and maybe we shouldn't have this and maybe we shouldn't have that. We decided in the end not to write up anything. There would not be any offense report of an aggravated battery on a law enforcement officer, nor any of the other charges. This also meant that we were not going to write up an injury report. We simply checked back into service and found someone else to arrest. At the end of the shift, I observed three softball sized bruises on my shoulder, my hip, and on my right calf.

***

I was dispatched to a call of an accident with injuries. While in route to the scene, we were advised that it was possibly a hit and run involving a white male suspect driving a full size Ford Econoline van. Upon arrival, we initially located a two tone Ford pick-up truck that had crashed into a concrete telephone pole. It turned out that the full size white Ford van had been traveling southbound on the street, when it struck the two tone Ford pick-up truck and fled from the scene. The impact from the white Ford van caused the Ford pick-up truck to strike a moped riding along the curb-line.

The moped was being operated by an 18 year old white male, with his girlfriend, a 15 year old white female on the back. The impact to the moped caused the 18 year old driver to be thrown off the moped onto the sidewalk virtually unharmed. The moped and the 15 year old passenger were both crushed into the concrete telephone pole by the Ford pick-up. The 15 year old female was killed instantly, was unrecognizable, and parts of her brain matter were crushed out of her skull.

We discovered from the boyfriend that the deceased's parents were on a trip out of state and she was not supposed to be out with him. Like many people, the teenage girl died simply because she was in the wrong place at the wrong time, some call that fate. We had to make our death notification through another law enforcement agency. There is no good way to deliver a death notification, so I would always simply tell people without hesitation. Breaking the news to someone slowly does not make it any easier. One thing that I would also do is triple check the information on the deceased and who you were to deliver the information to. It was also a good idea to have a little information on the scene of the death, because the family and friends always had many questions.

On the same evening of the teenage girl's death, we were able to obtain enough information from a witness to identify a full sized, white Ford van that was registered in another city in Florida. Officer M took that information and was able to generate an associated address, which was not far from the accident scene. We responded to that residence and located the white Ford van in the driveway. The van had the front end jacked up, had a utility light shining on it, and had some damage to the front end from the hit and run. The suspect was already trying to "fix" what he had done. We approached the front door of the residence to see if we could observe a suspect that matched the description provided. Through the window we could see the suspect, the white male registered owner, and a naked female that was later identified as his girlfriend. The suspect was arrested and eventually charged with DUI manslaughter.

The wheels of justice sometimes do tend to turn very slowly. A few years later, I obtained some follow up information on this case. The suspect sat in jail for a long time awaiting his trial. Eventually, the bond on his offense was lowered enough that the suspect was able to talk his mother into posting the equity in her home to get him bonded out. The suspect and the girlfriend fled out of town for a couple of years and had violated the bond. For whatever reason, they came back to the area and were staying in a motel on the beach. They made a suicide pact and the girlfriend called her own mother to say goodbye. Her mother was able to get enough information out of her daughter to send the police to stop the suicides. The original suspect was arrested for the active warrant from the DUI manslaughter charge and finally went to trial, was convicted, and sentenced.

***

At one point during that first year, I had to ride with one of the department's accident vans in the traffic unit. The accident vans were police officers with specialized training that would respond to any accident involving death or great bodily harm. I was assigned with Officer G for one week. We happened to be in the area of a dispatched call of a strong arm robbery from a Beall's Department store where the suspect left on foot. The loss prevention personnel had chased the suspect into a trailer park.

Upon our arrival, we took a position to the west on a perimeter and the K-9 unit was starting to track from the east side almost two blocks away. We had only been parked for about 30 seconds when the described white male suspect came trotting out from between two trailers. The suspect came right up to the front of our full-sized van I assume he did not expect it to be a police cruiser. I jumped out of the passenger seat and yelled, "Police, get on the ground." The suspect turned quickly and ran back in between the trailers. I began a foot pursuit after the suspect and was calling my direction of travel over the radio. I had assumed that the K-9 officer was not close, because he had started on the east side of the trailer park. The old saying is true, "when you assume you make an ASS out of U and ME".

The suspect was only about 15 feet in front of me when he turned northbound. I started to call his change of direction when I saw a flash of something run in front of me (the K-9). I was running full speed and was making the northbound cut when I ran into the K-9's lead and then directly into the K-9 officer holding the lead and running from the south. The impact took both of us to the ground, but the K-9 officer held onto the

26

lead, which caused the K-9 to jerk backward. The K-9 turned around to see me on the ground with his best friend in the world. I knew I was going to get bit, I just wasn't quite sure where. As the K-9 ran up, I simply curled into a ball on the ground and he bit onto my handcuff case and then partially onto my ass, of course! The suspect was caught and arrested and we ended up laughing it off.

***

One unusual call that I remember was being dispatched to a call of a late reported sexual battery. The victim had come to the lobby of the police station to report that she was the victim of sexual offenses that occurred 25 years ago when she was a child. I took the time to document the facts as remembered by the victim and research all of the potential hearsay witnesses and the suspect. I presented the case to an assistant state attorney and had the victim present for her testimony. Under the current law, some of the offenses classified as capital sexual battery. The assistant state attorney explained that he would have to go back and research what the law and statute of limitations were back when the offenses were committed. The victim advised that the only reason that she had come forward was she had heard that the suspect was going to be released from prison on other, unrelated offenses, and she did not want anyone else to become a victim. The state attorney's office was able to confirm that the suspect was not going to be released anytime in the near future and the victim decided not to pursue anything further with her case.

***

I responded to a call of "check welfare". Depending on the information provided these calls can frequently turn into calls involving a death. On this call, dispatch advised that a neighbor in a large apartment building was calling for us to check on an apartment with the door ajar. The neighbor advised that an "old man" lived in the unit and he had not been seen today. Upon arrival, I noticed that the morning newspaper was on the floor outside his door and the door was ajar resting on the latch. I knocked, announced my presence and entered the unit.

Once inside, I found the subject deceased. The subject was a 91 year old white male who lived alone and did not have any family in the state. The deceased had carefully laid out a few of his financial documents and had included a hand written note. The overall theme of the note was that the deceased's health had deteriorated to a point where he did not want to live anymore and there was great desperation in his words. The date was December 29 and it is true that many people commit suicide in the month of December. The deceased had taken a clear plastic bag and placed it over his head and then tied a blue men's necktie around his neck to make the bag airtight. This was a sad and lonely scene.

***

I made it through the remainder of my first year and had to attend an end of probation board. I had to sit before my entire chain of command up through the assistant chief. There were only four officers hired from my academy class, but only two of us (50%) made it through the first year. Officer W had problems with report writing, while in the FTO unit, and was let go. Officer K had an incident with too much liquid courage while off duty and was in a confrontation in a bar with a State of Florida ATF agent. Officer K ended up being fired prior to the end of probation. Over the course of my career, there were many officers that lost their career due to alcohol or women. They say the badge will get the women, but the women will take the badge!

Officer H and I each had our separate board interviews and were informed that we each had made it through the probationary first year. At the end of my board interview, I was asked, "if you were chief for a day what would you change about your first year?" A question like this one needs to be answered very carefully, so you don't step on anyone's toes. I chose to address something outside of simply the procedures of my first year. I explained to the board that patrol officers generated many cases where probable cause was issued for the arrest of known suspects, and the probable cause eventually leads to arrest warrants issued from the state, but no one in our department focused on finding and arresting these suspects. A few years later, there were two different specialized units formed to focus attention on arresting wanted suspects, for both juveniles and adults that seemed to fill that void.

Chapter 5

I was feeling very comfortable in my role as a police officer. I was still working a late evening shift and our patrol division still worked five eight hour days per week. If you were a hard worker, there was also plenty of overtime. I drove to work in my personal vehicle, so I always dressed into my uniform in the locker room at work. From the very beginning of my career, I made a point to keep my home life and my work life separate. I never brought home any stories about what happened during my shift and getting dressed into my uniform at work was just one little way of keeping that separation. I can remember getting an almost giddy feeling as I finished getting dressed into my uniform wondering what kind of "trouble" I could stir up that day. On more than one occasion, I stated, "If I had no bills, I would do this job for free!"

The department had 540 sworn officer positions and approximately 200 civilian positions. I made a point to become friends with everyone. I went out of my way to get to know patrol officers on different shifts and in different districts and also to get to know various supervisors and all of the detectives. I observed right away that there were some officers that did not treat civilian employees the same as they did fellow officers. I made a point to be friends with everyone, because I knew that we were all on the same team. I treated everyone at work with the same respect and was equally friendly with the janitors as I was with the Chief of Police.

Another area that I made a point to get involved with was trying to make the department moral better. Just like in any other job, police officers like to feel appreciated and part of that appreciation comes from earning comparable pay and benefits to other near-by police agencies. During my first year, I met with Officer S, who was the president of the police union at the time.

NO ONE got along with Officer S and I think he made a point to always come across as abrasive as he could. I had no problems with Officer S and spoke to him on many occasions about pay and benefits and how the union contract worked. The union negotiated a new contract every three years with the city, but the union really did not have a whole lot of bargaining power.

I was not able to get onto the contract negotiating team during my first year, but I kept informed during that process and joined after my first year continuing up until the final contract of my career. I wanted to make improvements in pay and benefits for all officers and spent a great deal of my personal time working on the team. Most of my involvement was looking for areas of improvement in the contract, interpreting what changes the city wanted to make, and publicizing spreadsheets of comparable pay and benefits from surrounding police agencies. During my career, the top officer pay increased by about 62% and we increased the pension payout from 50% of pay up to 75% of an officer's pay.

***

In policing, you never know what piece of information you may obtain from someone that becomes a crucial piece of information to a future investigation. What may seem like trivial information at the moment could actually be very important. Therefore, it is imperative for police officers to document everything.

As an example, I conducted a traffic stop on a vehicle for improper or unsafe equipment for having one of the headlights inoperable. The black male driver of the vehicle advised that he did not have a valid driver's license. The vehicle that he was driving was a 1991 white Toyota Tercel that he had borrowed from his girlfriend. I placed the driver under arrest and asked him if he had a phone number for the registered owner of the vehicle. The arrested driver provided the number, so that I would not have to tow the vehicle. The registered owner responded to the scene and I verified her identity and documented her information onto my notepad. However, when I typed my arrest report, I failed to include the owner's address and phone number.

A few months later, that same black male suspect walked up to a 47 year old armored car driver and shot him in the back of his head without any warning. The armored car driver had three children, was retired military, and had only been working that job for seven weeks. The black male suspect had been identified through witnesses, but had not been located. I received a call from Homicide Detective G and he questioned me about the traffic stop. I advised Detective G that I had the girlfriend's information on my old notepad at my home. I drove the marked cruiser home and located the notepad. The black male suspect was later located and arrested.

***

Since I almost always worked in the inner-city, I usually conducted traffic stops to go after criminal violations. Each and every stop that I made was for a valid traffic violation, but I hoped that it would lead to bigger crime. I never really worked traffic with the intent of making the roadways safer or to try and write a certain number of tickets. Early in my career, the department sent everyone to "radar school" to learn how to operate a speed radar gun. Soon after that, the laser gun became the more reliable device and I had to attend a training school for the laser gun. I never wrote a single ticket using either device in my entire career.

I guess I did write a couple citations in the name of safety. I wrote one individual a citation for unsafe equipment when I observed that his driver's seat was a five gallon gas can that he had a fuel line coming out of that went straight to the engine.

On another occasion, I stopped a female when I observed several children jumping around in her vehicle. I saw a black female driving a large four door vehicle, with all of the windows down, and three children jumping around in the car. I approached the female and spoke to her about her children wearing seatbelts and being in child safety seats. Technically each child not in a seat was a separate violation and a separate $80 ticket. I knew that if I even gave her one ticket there would be even less of a chance she could purchase child safety seats. I ran her license and registration and everything came back as valid, so I returned to her with a pamphlet that described how she could get free child safety seats if she qualified as a low income resident.

During my explanation, there was a 2 year old toddler that was literally jumping up and down on the back seat telling the mother that he was hungry. The driver was an extremely fat female and she had on a very baggy shirt. While I was standing at the driver's door making my explanation, the driver stated, "If you hungry baby come up here and get you some." The child leapt over the back of the front seat and approached the mother. The driver then lifted up her shirt to reveal a breast that was hanging all the way down to her waist. The child grasped the breast with both hands and latched on to it. I could see that my education on safety was not going anywhere and simply told the woman, "If you love your children, you will put them in safety seats" and I left.

**

Domestic related calls are any calls involving some sort of dispute between individuals that are currently or had lived together in a domestic relationship as a family. These calls can be simple verbal disagreements or they could be criminal offenses like assaults, batteries, or homicides. Officers truly never know what situation they are walking into with domestic calls. People spend years in deteriorating relationships and then expect officers to solve all the problems in the fifteen minutes that the officer is in their home.

I remember responding as a back-up unit to one domestic call that involved shots fired. Two calls came into communications through the 911 system. The first call was from the suspect's wife, who advised that her husband chased her sister out of their home with a gun and fired several shots. The second caller was the sister who called from a neighboring house. The sister advised that she was chased out of her sister's home by her brother-in-law, and she believed that he may have shot his wife (her sister). Both callers had indicated that they believed the opposite sister had been shot. Upon arrival, I located the wife, or first caller, at the residence where the shooting occurred and obtained her statements. The suspect had fled the scene in his vehicle, so a "be on the look-out" (BOLO) was issued over the radio.

The wife advised that they had moved to Florida from Texas four days prior to this offense. The wife advised that there had been constant fighting and her husband, the suspect, had left yesterday and returned late this evening. The wife advised that the suspect came into the home screaming at her sister, pulled a gun out, and stated, "I came here to end it all". The wife advised that the suspect chased her sister out of the house, fired several shots, and then fled the scene. The sister was located at a neighbor's house and brought back to the scene of the offense. In the driveway out in front of the residence, we located five shell casings and observed that several rounds had been fired into the sister's vehicle. A technician responded to photograph the victim's injuries and the scene. We stood by as the two sisters gathered their belongings, the wife's two children, and watched them leave to stay in a hotel.

Six years later I received a subpoena to appear for a deposition on this case. Prior to walking into the deposition, I was briefed by the assistant state attorney (ASA). The ASA advised that the original suspect in this offense tracked down the wife and his two children in Utah about a year later and kidnapped the children from her and had planned to kill her and dispose of her body. The suspect was arrested in Utah and had items like a shovel, duct tape, plastic, and a bag of cement in his trunk. I do not recall the specific charges that he was convicted of, but he served five years in Utah. At the end of his Utah sentence, the Florida warrant for the suspect's arrest was served and he was extradited to stand trial in Florida. After the extradition, a judge granted the suspect a bond and he had bonded out on these charges. An unusual part of the case was the suspect was going to be representing himself in court. Usually, they say that a suspect who represents themselves has a fool for a client.

At the trial, I learned that the State of Florida had a couple devastating blows to their case. The wife of the suspect was too afraid to come out of hiding to testify at the trial and the photographic evidence of the scene was destroyed by the records division of the police department. I learned that the records division supervisor assumed that there was a five year statute of limitations on the offense and put the photographic evidence in for destruction. The sister-in-law did show up for the trial, but the jury decided the suspect was not guilty. Believe it or not the suspect was at trial with his new "wife" that he met while in prison in Utah. I assumed that she would be a future victim.

***

I responded to a call of an aggravated battery that was domestic related. Upon arrival, I found the suspect had fled the scene on foot, so I had my back-up unit circulate for him. I spoke to the victim and she refused any need for rescue units. The victim advised that another black female came by her residence and called her a "bitch". The victim advised that she asked her live-in boyfriend why he let the other female call her a bitch. The victim advised that the two of them started to argue and she told him that his deceased mother was a "bitch". At that point, the suspect, boyfriend, punched the victim in the mouth knocking out her top center right front tooth. I felt bad for the 38 year old victim because I knew she would have a permanent disfigurement for the rest of her life. The punch didn't just break her tooth off it knocked the entire tooth out from the root. I never realized just how big a human front center tooth could be.

***

I was dispatched to a call of a battery. Upon arrival, I spoke with the victim a 69 year old white female. The female advised that she was out walking her "police trained" five year old German shepherd. She advised that she observed her neighbor's small dog running loose on the street and her German shepherd pulled away from her and attacked the small dog. The German shepherd held the small dog in his mouth and shook it from side to side. She advised that her neighbor came out and kicked her dog and then punched her in the upper arm. The victim showed a visible bruise to her upper arm, but it was hard to determine if it could have come from a punch. The neighbor, suspect, was actually an attorney and denied punching the victim. There appeared to be an ongoing dispute between the two neighbors. I had to present the case to an assistant state attorney because a battery to an individual over 65 years of age is a felony in Florida. State attorney's hate cases like this because of all of the politics involved and it's damned if you do or damned if you don't file a charge. The case was not very strong because there were no independent witnesses, and the state attorney was able to talk the victim out of her desire to prosecute.

***

My youngest arrest of a suspect actually dealing in narcotics was a ten year old black male. I had initially checked out with the suspect to confirm that he wasn't a runaway juvenile that I had just taken a report about. The ten year old black male suspect had a large clear bag with 16 individual baggies of marijuana stuffed down the front of his pants. The suspect was arrested and transported to the juvenile assessment center. It was no surprise to learn that this was not his first offense and at age ten he was already listed as a habitual juvenile offender in the county.

***

As a police officer, if you work the same area long enough you really get to know the area's residents. Many times the victims of yesterday become the suspects in future cases. During one shift, I responded as a back-up unit to a domestic disturbance at a McDonald's. During the investigation of the domestic, I was approached by a five year old black male that advised that he witnessed the offense. The black male continued to advise that he was alone and had been living on the street because no one was home at his house.

I responded to his residence with him and, surprise, no one was home. I left a business card, called a state child abuse investigator, and took the juvenile to the police station. The child neglect case would later be presented to the State Attorney's Office and the call that night took almost five hours to resolve.

The reason that the call was even memorable was the fact that all of the children and the mother became involved as suspects in a strong arm robbery case 14 years later. The innocent five year old child abuse victim grew up to become my strong arm robbery

38

suspect. He pulled an 86 year old female to the ground in order to steal her purse as she was going to a doctor's office. The fall caused the elderly victim's hip to break and doctors initially thought that she would not survive the offense. The black male and his co-defendants were all arrested for a number of robberies.

***

It is hard for me to remember the actual first time that I was battered by a suspect while working in the capacity as a police officer. I sustained numerous injuries while arresting various suspects. The majority of time suspects are fighting to get away from you and not actually fighting to hurt you, but never assume they won't. By this explanation, I am talking about suspects that tense up, refuse to put their hands behind their back, pull their hands away from an officer, flee on foot, etc. There are other cases where a suspect will physically touch or strike a police officer prior to or during the actual arrest of the suspect.

One of the earliest battery offenses against me occurred on a "trouble with individual" call. Officer G and I arrived on scene and were attempting to determine who was involved or causing a problem. An 18 year old black male came walking up toward us yelling, "What's up?" several times in a row. The black male was putting on a show for the many witnesses that were out on both sides of the street.

I attempted to explain to the black male that we were called out to the scene. The black male continued to be extremely vocal and was waving his arms and hands all over the place and walked directly up toward me. The black male intentionally pushed me back on my chest and right shoulder area with the back of his forearm, as if he were showing the crowd who was in charge. I immediately pushed the black male back with a strong palm strike to the center of his chest. As the suspect fell to the ground away from me, the back of my hand

39

caught on the suspect's long gold chain necklace that was hanging low and popped it off of his neck, causing it to fly through the air. We took the suspect into custody and placed him into handcuffs. I am not certain if we ever determined why we were called to the scene.

Chapter 6

A residential burglary occurs when your family goes to work and then a suspect goes to work on breaking inside your home and taking your stuff. Police officers respond to thousands and thousands of residential burglaries every year. The majority of the time the calls are late reported and an officer or detective hopes to eventually obtain evidence to arrest a suspect.

At the start of my evening shift, I was dispatched to a call of a late reported residential burglary. The victim's residence was a two story wood frame apartment building with an exterior stairwell that led to the victim's second floor apartment. Halfway up the stairwell was a six pane window that led into the victim's living room. The window was the point of entry for the suspect when committing the burglary. I documented the scene and the property that was taken during the offense and also spoke to neighboring residents. I called a technician to respond and attempted to get any additional evidence. Technician P responded to process the scene. Technician P was pretty much at the end of his career and had a hell of a dry sense of humor.

The victim watched Technician P very intently as Technician P climbed the exterior stairwell, dusted the window pane, and lifted an entire handprint from where the suspect pushed the window open. Technician P put the fingerprint tape onto a white card, held the card up to view the print, and then turned the card sideways to look at it in a different angle. Technician P then looked the victim right in the eyes and asked, "Do you know an Anthony?" The victim immediately screamed out, "I knew it; that mother fucker; that's my brother-in-law". Technician P walked away from the scene without a smile and without saying another word. What are the odds of that being the right name to upset her?

***

I responded as a back-up unit to an accident that occurred at an intersection with a traffic signal. Upon arrival, I learned from the driver that had run through the red light that he was actually trying to get away from another individual that was chasing him in a car with a handgun. I informed Officer S that I would handle the aggravated assault offense and he could continue with his accident investigation. After we had finished investigating both incidents, Officer S came up to the victim of the aggravated assault and was issuing him a traffic citation for running the red light and causing the crash. The driver exclaimed, "You are giving me a ticket; I was running from a man with a gun". Without hesitation, Officer S stated, "Sir, I don't care if you were running from Satan chasing you with a bloody cycle, you ran the red light and caused an accident". Although I did not agree 100%, that impromptu statement was one of the best.

I followed up on the aggravated assault investigation and was able to generate a suspect through a street name provided by a witness. I showed the victim a photo pack and he was able to select the suspect, so I issued probable cause for his arrest for the aggravated assault. I was able to determine that he worked for the City and I arrested him as he drove away from his shift at the water department. I was hoping to recover the firearm from his vehicle, but that was never located.

***

I think the average citizen would be shocked at the number of drivers that run from a traffic stop, either on foot or in their vehicle. This offense is called fleeing and eluding and is a third degree felony in the State of Florida when the driver is being stopped by a marked police cruiser with lights and siren activated. It would not be surprising if there were at least two fleeing and eluding offenses on every evening shift. Normally, the suspect driver is fleeing from law enforcement for more than trying to avoid a traffic citation and the suspect always drives away in a reckless manner, disregarding traffic control devices, and putting other citizens in danger. In many cases, it is not worth the risk of killing an innocent motorist to catch a suspect that is fleeing and eluding, so I do agree with some restrictions on police officer pursuits.

I worked in a uniformed patrol capacity for a total of six and a half years and personally had a couple hundred of these offenses. I almost always made a point to document the offense in a police report and attempted a follow-up investigation, if I was able to obtain a tag number from the vehicle that fled. Many times the driver of the vehicle had borrowed the vehicle from a parent, girlfriend, or friend and if you make contact with the owner quick enough they do not have time to make up a story about who had their vehicle. Other times the suspects are driving rental vehicles that were rented in someone else's name, and if a vehicle is stolen it is almost guaranteed to flee from any traffic stop.

Officer D and I had a couple of offenses of fleeing and eluding with two black male cousins. On one incident, I attempted to stop a 1989 dark purple Chevy Caprice driven by Suspect O for an inoperable light. I initiated the traffic stop and Suspect O accelerated away from me, ran through a stop sign, and then pulled his vehicle over three blocks away from my cruiser. I had already turned off my lights and siren and stopped on the side of the road, but since I could see that Suspect O stopped I moved up and arrested Suspect O.

Suspect O advised that he fled from the traffic stop because he did not want to pull over in front of a couple females on the side of the road. Another time Suspect O fled in the same vehicle from Officer D and we were able to locate and arrest him later. On this offense, we decided to seize his vehicle under the State of Florida

Asset and Forfeiture Act. At the time the department policy was for officers to drive the seized vehicle to the impound yard. The vehicle had huge chrome rims and a stereo that was worth ten times the value of the vehicle. Officer D drove the vehicle around the neighborhood a couple times with Suspect O's cd playing extremely loudly through the open car windows. We will just say everyone in the neighborhood knew that Suspect O's vehicle was seized that day.

***

I attempted to pull a vehicle over on a traffic stop, but the vehicle's driver refused to stop and fled from the scene. This traffic stop was for some traffic infraction, so I shut off my lights and siren and requested a report number to document the offense.

Later in my shift, I was approached by Sergeant M who asked me if I knew who was driving the vehicle. When I advised "no", the Sergeant M continued and asked why I took a number to write a police report. I explained to the sergeant that many times when a felony is committed the suspect is not known and a report is still written. I provided the example of a case of a bank robbery where the suspect is not known and you write a police report to document the offense. The sergeant put up an argument that I was wrong for writing a police report, so I stated, "since the felony occurred in my presence, I assumed that I should document it in a police report". The sergeant still didn't understand or agree with me.

***

On another shift, Officer D spotted a vehicle that was listed as stolen in NCIC/FCIC, so he initiated a traffic stop. The vehicle pulled into an "L" shaped alley. Officer D had pulled into the alley behind the stolen vehicle and I had pulled into the alley at the opposite end. The suspect stopped the vehicle, jumped out, and ran on foot toward my position. Officer D began chasing the suspect on foot and I was running toward both of them. As the suspect was running he was watching Officer D over his shoulder. I hit the suspect with probably my best open field tackle of my lifetime and planted him into the ground. All of this played out right in front of an elderly black male sitting on his rear porch off of the alley. Upon the sight of the take down, the elderly man jumped to his feet and exclaimed, "Oh, my God I thought you kill't him".

***

I responded as a back-up unit to assist other officers in locating a white male fleeing and eluding suspect that had run on foot from a stolen vehicle. Officer D and I responded to a known address of a white male auto thief that lived in that immediate area. Upon arrival at that residence, we observed three angry dogs inside the fenced front yard of the residence. The front door of the residence was open, but no one responded to my yells. I entered the gate and one of the large dogs charged at me, so I sprayed him with pepper spray. The spray caused all three dogs to run away from me. I was able to make contact with the suspect's father, who was inside and intoxicated. The father stated something about his dogs biting Officer D, and Officer D told the father, "If your dog bites me I am going to punch you right in the mouth". Officer D said this out of frustration. I laughed to myself and diffused the situation by asking Officer D to go around and cover the rear door. I searched the residence with another officer, but did not locate the suspect that day.

On another offense with this same suspect, officers chased him on foot on an interstate overpass. When officers were about to catch him, the suspect jumped 30 feet to the roadway below breaking his hip in three different places and costing the same drunk father about $20,000 in medical bills.

***

We were very busy one evening shift, but I observed a vehicle driving recklessly through a residential neighborhood. I initiated a traffic stop on the vehicle, which pulled directly into a driveway. The black male driver immediately jumped out and ran southbound. Since we were so busy I knew that I wouldn't have any back-up units, so I decided that I wouldn't even chase him on foot. I was simply going to impound the car and investigate it later. The suspect had obviously fled from the police in the past, because he assumed that I was chasing him on foot. The suspect ran all the way around the house that he had stopped at and then right past my cruiser that I was sitting inside.

Since the suspect had already been running, I knew he was tired and would be easy to catch. I jumped out of my cruiser and caught and arrested the suspect within a half block.

***

I was driving southbound on a busy street and observed a black four door Chevy pull onto the roadway several blocks in front of me. As I drove closer to the vehicle, the driver changed lanes into the median lane and then quickly turned left into a driveway. I passed the vehicle, but continued watching it in my mirror. The driver kept his foot on the brake until I was almost out of sight and then quickly backed out of the driveway and drove back northbound. I turned my cruiser around to at least run the tag on the Chevy.

As I approached the Chevy that was now driving northbound, the driver made a quick left turn into a neighborhood and appeared like he was accelerating away from me. I initiated the lights and siren on my cruiser and the vehicle continued on its' same path but slowed to approximately thirty miles per hour. I observed the driver's door of the vehicle open as the vehicle continued. I advised the dispatcher that I needed a back-up unit, because it appeared like the suspect may flee on foot. I assumed the driver would stop the vehicle quickly and run away from it on foot.

The next thing I see is the black male driver jump out of the vehicle that was still traveling at thirty miles per hour and I see him sliding down the asphalt on his hands and knees. I am laughing so hard that I could barely tell other officers what just occurred. I observed the suspect jump to his feet and run off northbound, but I had to stay with the vehicle to ensure that it didn't kill anyone. The vehicle continued in a straight path and struck a tree, where there was a slight curve in the roadway.

I contacted the owner of the vehicle, who tried to claim that it stolen, but it sounded like the owner had trader her vehicle for crack cocaine. I never learned who the black male, suspect was, but knew that he would have two large circular scars, one on each knee.

***

I was dispatched to the scene of a death, where a 28 year old white male was found dead in his back yard. The caller was the wife of the deceased, who came home and found him in the back yard. The wife advised dispatch that he had been attacked and was missing his nose. The fire rescue units had arrived prior to me and had already pronounced the husband deceased.

Upon my arrival, I walked through the house and into the rear yard to observe a fully clothed young looking man lying on his back with his nose missing. There was almost no blood and except for the nose, it looked as if the man had simply lain down in this position. The fire rescue units advised for me not to touch anything, because their initial theory was that he could have been electrocuted and the electricity leaving the body caused the nose to blow off of his face. The deceased had been working on his yard irrigation system and had a small PVC elbow joint in one of his hands. The initial theory was quickly disproven because we could not find any evidence that he was also working on anything with electricity.

Eventually, after speaking with the wife, we learned that she walked into the back yard and found her husband in this position with two three month old puppies running around him. The wife had removed the puppies and enclosed them into the bathroom inside the house. We came to the conclusion that the puppies had eaten the nose from the man's face after he had died. Initially, I am sure the puppies were attempting to get the man's attention to play, which eventually lead to small nips, licking, and eventually the nose was entirely eaten off of the dead man's face.

By the time we had figured this out, there were several family members at the scene. I had a back-up officer that had prevented any of the family or friends from coming into the rear yard and observing the deceased. The deceased's mother had made several requests to see her young son and I promised her that I would allow it prior to the body being removed. The Medical Examiner's team arrived, put the deceased in the body bag, and I had them take the body around the side of the house to avoid the family. Next, I simply apologized to the mother and informed her that her son had been removed from the scene. No parent should have to observe their child at the scene of death in that condition. I knew the funeral home could prepare the body and mom would get her closure there without the horrible memory of the missing nose. I know that I made the right decision.

Chapter 7

Probation is a program that is painted as a second chance for people convicted of crimes. I believe part of the reason that it was created was the prison systems were overwhelmed. Probation used to be utilized for petty crimes or misdemeanor offenses and would be used instead of jail time. The probation itself was the punishment and therefore the defendant was under specific rules or conditions that they could not violate. Every defendant agrees or accepts the punishment of probation and the terms in court instead of being sentenced to incarceration. I certainly have nothing against giving someone a second chance, but the majority of defendants on probation were on their fifth or sixth chance and run about society like a child that has never been spanked or corrected. It is also always proven true that 10% of the people commit 90% of the crime, so not putting suspects in jail sometimes causes more crime.

The way probation was designed and the way that the judges utilized it was totally different. A defendant after being found guilty of a felony crime could be granted probation instead of prison, as long as the defendant abided by the restrictions and terms of probation. When the defendant violated probation, they were supposed to be resentenced to prison by the judge under the original sentencing guidelines. Judges, however, would be presented a case of a clear violation of probation and would simply resentence defendants to the same probation or extend the probation for a longer time period. I even heard judges make silly statements like, "Well, you have not been arrested for any other crimes." I interpreted this as the judge saying, "You had not been caught committing other crimes and I will ignore the crime of violation of probation."

As soon as a defendant violates his probation, by failing a drug test, missing meetings with their probation officer, leaving the jurisdiction, etc. they have committed another crime, a violation of probation. Once a defendant knew that they had violated probation, they would usually "go on the run" from law enforcement and when you are on the run anything goes. There are defendants that violate probation and then stay on the run for years, until they are finally caught committing other crimes. Defendants know that they are in violation of probation the moment they stop going to mandated meetings with their probation officer.

I always thought the State of Florida had it backward they put the responsibility of the violation of probation on the probation officer and by that I mean the probation officer was required to track down and arrest the defendant for a violation and prove the case in court. All this method did was created a probation system that was also overwhelmed. I believe that defendants should have the responsibility to prove they have abided by the terms of probation to the court and serve day for day in prison after they commit any violation of probation. Aren't the defendants the one being punished for committing crimes? From the first missed probation meeting, defendants are on the run, so the clock starts on that day. For every day that they are on the run, they should be sentenced to a day in prison and then resentenced for the original crimes. Treating probation like a privilege and not a right will put the "correction" back into the Department of Corrections.

***

In December of my second year, I received my first official discipline from the City. I always used to joke that you weren't a true cop unless you have been suspended at least once.

I initiated a traffic stop on a 1990 silver Mercury and the vehicle pulled over onto the sidewalk of a busy corner gas station. The suspect, driver, initially advised that he did not have his driver's license on him and that the vehicle belonged to a friend of his. The suspect provided the name of "Damion Mickel Sowers" and confirmed that spelling. I always found it funny to have suspects try to spell the alias names that they pretended to be. I verified that there was not any driver's license under the name provided and went back to the driver to place him under arrest for no valid driver's license. However, I knew that the suspect had provided a false name.

I opened the suspect's driver door, reached for his left arm, and asked him to step out of the vehicle. The suspect pushed my arm back with his left hand as he took his right hand and put the vehicle into drive. The suspect accelerated quickly off of the sidewalk leaving a 14 foot tire mark and recklessly drove through a red light at the intersection. Officer D and I followed in the suspect's path for four blocks and then observed him run from the vehicle on foot. We responded to where the suspect fled from the vehicle, located the female passenger running on foot, and impounded the vehicle. I positively identified who the suspect was and found him to have five outstanding warrants for his arrest.

I conducted further investigation on locating the suspect and found his location in a neighboring jurisdiction. Two nights later I met with two sheriff's deputies and had them check that location for the suspect. The suspect was located, arrested on the warrants, and found to be in possession of crack cocaine. For all of our efforts, we received official written discipline for initially following after the suspect when he fled in the vehicle. For all of the suspect's efforts, he received five years in a Florida prison.

***

I responded as a back-up unit to a call of an armed robbery to a Save N Pac grocery store. I was the first officer to arrive on scene and two female clerks unlocked the doors. I obtained initial statements from the clerks and put out a description of the suspect. The clerks were almost certain that it was an acquaintance "Lucky" that robbed the store and they knew him to work at an Albertson's grocery in the area. One of the clerks called her boyfriend, who worked at Albertson's, and he told her that "Lucky called in sick tonight". Once the control officer arrived on scene, I left and responded to the Albertson's to speak with the manager.

Upon arrival to the Albertson's, I observed a subject fitting the description of "Lucky" walk inside the front doors of Albertson's. I went inside and met with the manager upstairs. I kept an eye on the store and observed the same subject walking toward the front exit of the store. I ran downstairs calling for a back-up unit and stopped "Lucky" as he reached his mother's van parked in the parking lot. I obtained "Lucky's" true identity and talked him into voluntarily responding with me to talk to detectives at the station. The control unit on the robbery offense was still developing the probable cause for the suspect's arrest and he was placed under arrest later that night for the robbery. I wonder if he has a new "street name" now.

***

I had worked a case in the past that involved a black male that committed a fleeing and eluding where he left his girlfriend behind. I was able to develop his identity and later arrest him. A couple of months later, I met with the girlfriend as a complainant on an unusual call. The girlfriend advised that she was being harassed by her natural father. The complainant advised further that he was trying to get additional rent money from her that she did not owe. She advised further that her father should not even be in the country because he was using a fictitious name. The complainant advised that her father left the USA, traveled to the country of Laos, faked his death, and came back to the USA under a

52

fictitious name. She did not know the exact name, but did tell me the location of a maroon van registered to him.

I traveled to the location of the van and ran the tag for owner information. The registered owner's name came back with a name of about 20 consonants in a row without any vowels in the spelling. I met with a detective in our undercover vice unit and passed the information on to him. I was advised not to type the information into a police report. I did not investigate this any further and never learned the outcome of the detective's continued investigation.

***

I obtained information from detectives that there were two sexual batteries that occurred to prostitutes in one neighborhood. I started working with undercover units that began looking for the unknown suspect and identified several subjects in the area for them. At approximately 2015 hours, a local resident called the police department and advised that there was a subject that may match the description of the sexual battery suspect in the alley. A couple of the undercover detectives began watching the suspect and they agreed. After just a few minutes, that suspect started acting suspicious in the alley, so Sergeant B advised for units to check out with him.

A couple of the undercover detectives attempted to walk up to him and the suspect began to run from them. All three of us initiated a foot pursuit after the suspect as he ran eastbound along the front yards of the avenue. The suspect started to yell, "Mamma, mamma help me", as he ran up to one house. We placed him under arrest on the front yard.

I learned later that the suspect had just moved to Florida from Mississippi and had a couple sexual battery offenses in Mississippi in which he was a suspect and he eventually partially admitted to the local offenses. The suspect was on several medications for his mental health issues.

***

I responded to a call of a stabbing. Upon arrival, I observed the victim lying on his stomach in the middle of the road with a common steak knife sticking out of his back and there were vehicles stopped in the street around him. The rescue units were arriving just a couple seconds after me and approached the victim. Initially, witnesses in the street advised that the suspect left in a black dodge pick-up truck southbound, so I had units in the area stop that vehicle. The truck ended up not being involved.

I spoke with a "witness", who had called 911. The witness advised that she was having problems with her husband, obtained an injunction against him, and he was served the injunction on that date. She advised further that just moments before the stabbing she was at home inside her apartment when her husband kicked the door down. The witness advised that her husband ran to the kitchen, grabbed two steak knives, and ran back outside. She advised that she did not observe the stabbing, because she was calling 911. The witness did advise that the steak knife in the victim's back was one of one's from her kitchen.

I sent Officer J to the hospital with the victim and I was still documenting the scene and speaking to other witnesses. Our communications center advised over the radio that the suspect had returned to the scene from the north. I assisted two other uniformed officers in placing the suspect under arrest and into my cruiser. I obtained statements from the suspect and his version was that the altercation between him and the suspect was more mutual combat.

I learned later what transpired at the hospital with the victim in surgery. The knife that was sticking into the victim's back was a common sized steak knife with an approximate five inch blade. The blade was stuck into the victim's back all the way to the off-white plastic handle. The stabbing actually occurred just three blocks from the local trauma hospital, what luck. A well-known ER surgeon, Dr. E, was called in to the hospital to treat the patient. Officer J advised that after the patient was prepped in the surgery room, Dr. E looked at the x-ray and approached the patient. Dr. E initially grabbed the knife and pulled, but he started to move the victim. Dr. E went back to the x-ray and looked at it. Dr. E then attempted another pull on the knife a second time, which separated the plastic handle from the metal blade that was still stuck into the victim's back. Dr. E then advised Officer J that he knew what he needed to get the knife out. Dr. E left the surgery room, went outside to his pick-up truck, and retrieved a pair of "Sears Robo-grip pliers". Dr. E then entered the surgery room and ripped the knife out of the victim's back with the pliers. The patient had a complete recovery.

***

I was dispatched to the trauma hospital to assist another agency with a boating accident. Upon arrival, the injured victim in the accident was just arriving by ambulance. The victim was a white male that was approximately 40 years old and had a massive head injury. The victim had been out with friends on his boat and was driving it under a bridge when the accident occurred. The victim was standing up driving the boat at a high speed and was turned around talking to friends. The moment the victim turned back to watch where he was driving, his head slammed into the concrete bridge.

I was surprised that the victim was even alive, when I observed his injury. The victim's head had hit a corner concrete support beam on the bridge and it literally left that imprint into the victim's face. The victim's upper left face was crushed into his skull, the eye was missing, and there was a 90 degree angle at the bottom of the victim's nose.

I went into one of the trauma rooms with the victim as the emergency room personnel prepped the victim for surgery and completed numerous scans. However, the victim ended up passing away prior to the start of any surgery.

***

Police officers are not only dispatched to crimes in progress. People call "911" or directly to the police department any time that they are not certain who else to call. In the county that I worked, all of the "911" calls went to one location and those operators were responsible for notifying the agency with jurisdiction, meaning the police or fire department in the correct city. Many of the calls that went to "911" were not even emergency calls and there were plenty of times that police officers were dispatched to non-criminal matters.

Many times officers are dispatched to calls with the fire department or with rescue units and they arrive to find the incidents are not criminal or are only medical problems. I remember being dispatched to many alligator calls, simply where a citizen observed an alligator that wasn't in the water. On another call, I responded to a tenant that had a hive of bees in the wall of his apartment that were extremely loud and getting inside. Police officers are not issued bee keeper suits.

As soon as there is any kind of argument or disagreement some people will call the police. Many disagreements are civil matters that ultimately would have to be settled by the parties themselves or in civil court. One of the main functions of a police force is to keep the peace and the mere presence of an officer normally accomplishes that purpose. Police officers are dispatched to plenty of calls such as neighborhood disputes, disorderly juveniles, trouble with an individual, etc. where the police officer arrives and determines if any criminal laws were committed. Many times the role of the police officer ends up being simply separating the subjects involved to keep the peace.

Chapter 8

Over the course of my police career, I ended up racking up an extensive injury history. I tried to only write up injuries that definitely required medical attention or could lead to long-term problems. I ended up on a first name basis with the doctors and nurses at the emergency room where we were required to go to, and also knew the City's worker's compensation representative very well. I lost count of the total number of individual injuries, but I did have a total of five different orthopedic surgeries for separate incidents. It seemed like there was at least one person every two weeks that would put up significant physical resistance or want to fight the police. I used to joke that there was always at least one physical confrontation that made me earn each and every paycheck.

***

I was working on patrol within my district, when I heard Officer C call over the radio that she had located an auto theft suspect and that she needed back-up units to respond. A moment later, there was a second transmission from Officer C and it sounded as if she were struggling with that suspect. I began to respond to her location with my lights and siren activated, and I wasn't real close to her location.

I was driving on a two lane road coming up a hill and there was one vehicle in the distance in front of me. I observed that vehicle slow and pull slightly off the edge of the roadway to the right and it appeared to be yielding to my emergency vehicle. I accelerated as I approached to pass that vehicle and I could feel the transmission downshift to a passing gear. My cruiser was going about 50 miles per hour as I started to pass that vehicle. The driver of that vehicle suddenly accelerated from a stopped position and attempted to turn left into an apartment complex at the exact moment I was starting to pass. His vehicle struck the

59

front fender of my cruiser causing my vehicle to head directly into the apartment parking lot. As I looked ahead of my cruiser, I could see a couple black females and at least two children playing in the middle of the parking lot. The entire complex was surrounded by a six foot masonry block wall. I turned my cruiser as fast as I could to the right to intentionally strike the corner pillar of the masonry block wall, which stopped my cruiser in its' path.

It is possible that I was knocked out for a split second. The first thing that I remember was a 20 year old black male at my driver's window yelling, "Holy shit, are you alright?" Ironically, he was probably one of the problem individuals from the complex that hung out and sold narcotics all day. I could see that the hood of the cruiser was now sticking up in the air about as high as the roof on my vehicle. I was looking through air bag dust, a broken windshield, and steam from the radiator exploding. I realized that the wind was still knocked out of me, as I could not breathe, yet, so I shook my head and let out a raspy, "I'm alright". I reached for my cruiser radio microphone and quickly realized that nothing was working in the vehicle. I keyed up the police radio on my hip and attempted to speak. I initially still could not breathe, but I stated, "314 Bravo I need rescue for a code 4 (accident) at Citrus Grove Apartments".

I am quite certain that my first attempt at communication was very low volume and not spoken too clearly. Everyone else in the patrol district was focusing on getting some help to Officer C, who was possibly physically struggling with an auto theft suspect. When an officer is calling for help, there is no need for anyone else to get on the radio and tie up the channel. The officer needing help may have to communicate something pertinent, so unless there is another emergency no other officer should be on the air. I heard

Officer S, another patrol officer, yell at me over the radio, "Keep the air clear, radio can you check on Officer C?" I realized I was going to have to try a little harder to get some help for myself. My second attempt at communicating over the radio came out a little clearer and the dispatcher acknowledged that she was sending rescue to me.

By the time rescue arrived, I had climbed out of my cruiser through my driver's door window as none of doors would open. I was pretty certain that my left leg was broken, but it ended up being a bone bruise near the knee. By this point, everyone at the apartment complex was enjoying the show, as there was a crowd of about 60 people standing in the parking lot. Other officers had arrived and they were attempting to locate the driver of the other vehicle. I looked into the center of the crowd and observed the driver, Suspect J, who was known to me and was the cousin of the previously mentioned Suspect O. I remembered a split second before impact looking into the face of the other driver as he was attempting that left turn. As I continued to look at Suspect J, I think he knew he was "caught" and he stepped forward and started to talk to Officer G.

The rescue personnel wanted me to get my money's worth, so they hooked me up to a back board and neck brace and let me ride in the ambulance. I found out later that Suspect J thought that I was pulling him over because he had a stolen tag on the vehicle he was driving. Suspect J was only 16 years old and also only had a restricted learner's license.

About five years later, Suspect J did a drive by shooting to a residence and killed an 8 year old female. Suspect J was convicted of that shooting and was sentenced to life in prison.

***

About six months later, an officer locates a stolen vehicle. I don't remember all of the details on the charges, but a pursuit was authorized. We end up chasing the vehicle all over the inner-city until it crashes over a curb at an intersection. I chased the suspect driver from the stolen vehicle as he and three passengers run on foot. The suspect ran southeast to a residence and jumped a four foot chain link fence into the rear yard. I had become pretty efficient at getting over chain link fences. I used to use the center of my chest, since I always wore a vest, to simply roll over the fence. In this foot pursuit, I only used my hands to jump the fence. Once over the fence, I started to continue running and was literally pulled backward by a piece of the metal fencing that had stuck into the palm of my hand. We were able to catch the suspect and I ended up with another trip to the emergency room and about six stitches in my right palm.

***

In read-off, we were provided information on a wanted subject that had possibly committed three recent armed bank robberies. There was probable cause for the suspect on one of the armed robberies. After read-off, I went directly to an area where a citizen had reported seeing the suspect. Upon arrival, I met with Sergeant L, who had the same idea.

We walked to the address and met with a black female, who advised that she had called earlier. The female advised that she saw the suspect leave a boarded up residence in a southbound direction approximately 30 minutes prior to our arrival. I left and went to an alley to the south of that location and called for Sergeant L to help me search two different boarded up residences. I exited my cruiser and started to approach the residences when I observed the suspect walking away in a northbound direction.

I notified other units over the radio that I had located the bank robbery suspect and started a foot pursuit after him. I yelled for the suspect to stop and get on the ground, but the suspect continued to run. The suspect basically looped around two different houses, so I had to keep changing my direction of travel over the radio. I caught the suspect in a rear yard prior to him jumping over another fence. The suspect stated, "Ok you got me man, don't hurt me!" The suspect was found to be in possession of crack cocaine and admitted to me that he had just finished smoking "crack" when I found him. The suspect also had in his possession a U.S. five dollar bill that was covered in dye from one of the dye packs exploding after the bank robbery.

***

Good cops are always looking to get involved in the action, such as a pursuit, an in-progress call, finding a wanted subject, etc. One evening shift at approximately 1900 hours a call comes in through 911 that there was a "carjacking" of a motorcycle from the victim's residence. At the time, I was working as a two man unit and had Officer L riding with me. We were not too far away from the victim's residence, so we raced to get there to confirm the carjacking just in case other units were to locate the suspects on the motorcycle.

While we were in route, Officer M advised that he had located the motorcycle at an intersection and it was heading northbound. Officer M advised that he initiated a traffic stop on the motorcycle, but the driver was not stopping. I knew that for a pursuit to be approved, an officer would have to confirm that the violent offense of carjacking did occur directly from the victim, so we continued to race to the victim's residence. Officer M requested approval for a pursuit over the radio and Sergeant L denied approval because the carjacking offense had not been confirmed yet. At that moment, I had run up to the victim's door and was banging on it to speak with him. The victim came out of the house through a side door under the carport and I yelled, "Hey did someone just take your motorcycle using a gun?"

The victim responded, "Yeah", and I advised on the radio that it was a confirmed carjacking.

It had only been about thirty seconds since the pursuit was denied, so Sergeant L advised units that if they located the motorcycle again a pursuit would be approved. Officer M advised right away that he thought that he could still see the motorcycle and it was getting on the interstate. Units began to pursue the motorcycle. I continued to get information from the victim and it was no shock to me to learn that the whole carjacking offense was related to narcotic activity. The victim advised that there was a group of subjects that came to his residence with guns in a black Ford Explorer. I relayed information to officers in the pursuit about the details of the Ford Explorer and the guns involved. Units in the pursuit lost sight of the motorcycle but were able to see the Explorer and pursue those suspects. The officers pursued the Explorer across a seven mile bridge into another jurisdiction. During the pursuit over the bridge, the suspects threw a handgun into the water and Officer W noted the number on the marker pole of the bridge for the location of the evidence.

The neighboring police department was informed of the offense and the pursuit, and they boxed the suspect vehicle to stop it. All of the suspects were arrested with the exception of the one on the motorcycle, who was caught at a later time. I drove the victim to the neighboring jurisdiction to identify all of the suspects. The next day the fire department's dive team recovered the handgun that had been thrown into the water.

***

Officer B was another great police officer that I enjoyed working with on the street. Officer B had been put in contact with a local newspaper reporter, who was trying to complete a series of stories on the problems with crack cocaine in the inner-city. The paper had made arrangements with the department for the reporter to ride with Officer B to complete her story.

We hit the street and started looking for crime. Within fifteen minutes, I observed a yellow taxi driving in circles within the zone. We observed a 40 year old white male ride up the taxi and purchase crack cocaine from a black male that was riding in the rear of the taxi. Officer B and Officer L stopped the white male suspect on his bicycle and developed probable cause for his arrest for possession of crack cocaine. The white male had hidden his crack cocaine rocks down in the cellophane wrapper of his cigarettes and had a glass crack cocaine pipe stuck down inside amongst the individual cigarettes.

I followed the yellow taxi away from the scene of the sale of the narcotics and initiated a traffic stop on the cab. The taxi driver stopped his vehicle and the black male rear passenger jumped out and ran southbound on foot in between the houses. I told the taxi driver to remain at the traffic stop and attempted a foot pursuit on the black male, but he was able to get away. Later that evening, I was able to establish the black male's true identity through a witness within my zone that knew his street name of "Tuck".

The newspaper reporter had allocated an entire shift to compile her story and Officer B and I were able to give her everything she needed within thirty minutes. The two page story was printed in the paper with about five pictures from the incident. Luckily, my name was left out and Officer B received full credit.

***

The department organized an operation that was supposed to last all summer long called the "Gun Abatement Program" or GAP. GAP was created to focus on all of the recent gun violence that had been happening at the time. Officers were advised that they were to focus on criminals with guns in an attempt to get as many guns off of the street as possible. The reality was that police officers simply focused on the active criminals, because almost all active criminals carried guns. The best part about the operation was everyone could work as a group and almost none of the criminals escaped arrest.

I was put on the operation as a back-up unit, so I coined myself a "bench warmer". I was utilized whenever one of the units assigned to the operation wanted or needed a day off. I ended up working with the operation about once per week. The police department needed the operation to be viewed as a success for political reasons and also to ensure citizens that the department was able to control the recent violence. For those reasons, the police officers were given the ability to combat criminals as aggressively as Florida State Statutes would allow. Some of these tactics granted a little more leniency than the police department's rules and regulations allowed at the time.

I was working with the operation one evening shift, and we had just finished arresting an individual with warrants and crack cocaine. I had the arrested suspect in the rear of my cruiser and was transporting him to the prisoner transport van at the rear of the station. I didn't want the suspect to hear anything that officers were saying over the cruiser's police radio, so I had changed the channel one down to a channel that was not being used. I could still hear everything with the operation in my earpiece from my portable radio on my hip.

All of the sudden, I hear Officer A shouting that he needed back up and that a suspect had battered him and he was bleeding. I was disappointed that I was not available to help since I had the other suspect, because I was not that far away. Seconds later, I realized that Officer A was calling for help over the radio channel on the cruiser and I was probably the only person on the department that was hearing him. It was simply dumb luck that I had changed the cruiser radio to that channel. Much of my career was built around dumb luck. I called over my portable radio to all of the other units working the operation and relayed Officer A's call for help as I turned my cruiser around to respond to assist. I notified Officer A on the cruiser radio that his portable radio had been knocked to the wrong channel and that I had help coming.

I arrived to the location of Officer A, which was the alley behind a half address. I observed a cut above Officer A's left eye that was bleeding down his face. Technically, I was violating some rules and regulations, because I had to leave my arrested suspect in the cruiser in the alley. I located Officer A at the entry door to the half address and he advised that his suspect had just run inside and locked the door. We were about to kick the door down and enter the half address, when a black female cracked the door open. We pushed past the female with a group of four officers and searched the tiny residence.

The suspect was located in the only bedroom and had jumped onto a single bed and was trying to pretend like he was asleep. As soon as we entered the room, we yelled commands for the suspect to show his hands and get on the floor. The suspect stood quickly up onto the bed and started swinging and flailing his arms toward officers. This response was a huge mistake. The four of us grabbed ahold of the suspect and planted him into the floor of the residence and handcuffed him.

I returned to my cruiser to find my original suspect waiting patiently and ended up transporting two prisoners to the rear of the station.

Chapter 9

I responded to several motorcycle accidents, which ended in fatalities. In fact, I really can't recall a motorcycle accident scene that I went to that wasn't a fatality. In Florida motorcycles have earned the name "donor-cycles". Early in my career, I went to the scene of a single vehicle accident, where a motorcyclist lost control and was basically dead at the scene, but was not pronounced until he reached the hospital. The deceased driver was racing the bike along a short straight away, when he lost control, hit the curb, and possibly broke his neck. The deceased did have a helmet on his head, which stayed on after impact.

Whenever there was a fatality accident, regular patrol officers simply secured the scene and called in one of the officers that worked the accident vans, due to the high civil liability involved. In this case, I had already secured the scene with crime scene tape and was waiting on the accident van. I was speaking with the brother of the deceased, who was with him at the time of his death. I specifically remembered the brother pushing to get custody of the motorcycle. I explained to him that the motorcycle would be impounded until the accident investigation was completed. The motorcycle had very minimal damage and possibly could have been driven away from the scene had there not been a death.

Approximately 18 months later, I responded as a back-up unit to another motorcycle fatality about one mile away. The brother was riding the same motorcycle and crashed at a high rate of speed into a city dump truck. The brother was killed and the motorcycle was totaled. The saddest untold part of the story is that the first brother, 27 years old, left behind six children and the second brother, 32 years old, left behind four children.

***

One night after my evening shift, I was heading home in my personal vehicle at approximately 0330 hours. I observed a 1996 blue Kia Sephia in front of me at a traffic light. The vehicle made a sudden westbound turn through the intersection, drove up onto the sidewalk, through a gas station parking lot, and then continued westbound. Next, the entire vehicle swerved into the oncoming lanes of traffic and then went back over the north curb to intentionally strike a traffic speed limit sign. The vehicle then continued, drove across the avenue, jumped the south curb to drive through a yard of the residence on the corner, went across a street, and then struck a fence of the residence on the opposite corner. I had fumbled to pull out my portable police radio and was calling in the driver's actions to get units to respond. It actually looked like I was watching a video game where the object of the game was to run into everything in sight.

At this point, I thought maybe the driver was finished, but then I observed the vehicle's back up lights come on. The vehicle backed away from the fence and accelerated quickly southbound on the street. The vehicle swerved back and forth and then accelerated into a blue truck parked in a driveway, which knocked it into a yellow Buick, also in that same driveway. The suspect driver wasn't finished, yet, and he continued striking everything in his path including a boat. Eventually, the suspect accelerated to a speed of about 50 miles per hour and drove into a parked car in a driveway. The suspect vehicle was inoperable and caught fire beneath the hood. I assisted the responding units in placing the suspect under arrest and called for rescue units to ensure he was not injured. The suspect was later found to have an active warrant and a suspended driver's license, but I never found out the reasons for his erratic driving.

***

On another evening shift, I had Officer H riding with me as a two man unit. We observed an old Brown Chrysler K car commit a traffic violation. I initiated a traffic stop on the vehicle that was being driven by an approximate 65 year old black male. We could see that the driver knew he was being stopped by our cruiser, but was not stopping his own vehicle right away. Next, as expected, we observed a small zip lock baggie come flying out the driver's window and fall onto the asphalt roadway under my cruiser. I quickly stopped the cruiser and let Officer H out to retrieve what was later found to be crack cocaine. I then continued driving after the suspect driver, who stopped about a half block away from the abandoned narcotics.

I was obtaining the driver's license, registration, and insurance card, when Officer H advised me that the discarded item was crack cocaine. I had the suspect step out of the vehicle and placed him under arrest for the narcotic. Upon a search incident to the arrest, I also located another small zip lock baggie containing three blue pills, Viagra. The suspect advised that he did not have a prescription for the "medicine", so I ended up submitting it into our narcotic destruction locker instead of charging him with another crime.

Even though the vehicle was not really worth any value, we seized it since it was used in the commission of the felony. The following day, I came to work and had a voicemail message from the suspect, who wanted to get his three Viagra pills back. The suspect was charged with a third degree felony of possession of cocaine, his vehicle was seized through the State of Florida Asset and Forfeiture Act, and three individual Viagra pills were seized and destroyed. The suspect obviously had only one concern on his mind.

***

My last name, Bizzell, is not extremely common. One evening, I responded as a back-up unit to Officer J on a traffic stop of a moped. Upon arrival, Officer J handed me the operator's driver's license and stated, "Look at that". I was surprised to see the name Bizzell. I obviously knew that we were not related because I know my family and the individual was a black male.

The moped ended up being stolen and the suspect was later found to be in possession of a misdemeanor amount of marijuana. The suspect was arrested and the owner of the moped was called to take possession of his moped. Many months later, I received a subpoena for trial. The motor vehicle theft of the moped must have been "dropped" by the assistant state attorney, but they were prosecuting on the misdemeanor marijuana.

I came to the county courthouse to testify to my actions and observations from that offense. There was a local law school that must have had an agreement with the state attorney's office to allow students to participate in criminal trials. I did have to testify in the trial and the judge actually assisted the student attorneys with their questioning and legal proceedings. Normally, the entire trial would have lasted about seven minutes total for a case as simple as this one. I personally was on the stand for over 30 minutes and they also had Officer J testify. The funniest part of the trial was watching the student attorney fumble with the question of whether I was related to the defendant, Bizzell. A few years later, that defendant's little brother and two other juveniles were killed in a stolen vehicle that crashed after fleeing from a police cruiser.

***

One evening shift, there was a request from one of the homicide detectives for marked cruisers to move into an area and stop a vehicle. The suspect, driver, was known to the detectives and he had intentionally swerved at their vehicle while driving. Officer D and I were not too far away, so we were the first to arrive in the area. The homicide detectives described the vehicle

72

and I pulled in behind it as it made a northbound turn. I activated my lights and siren on the cruiser to conduct a traffic stop and the suspect vehicle began to flee. About a block ahead, I could see one other vehicle on the road and it had just put on its' left turn signal.

I shut down the lights and siren and pulled to the side of the road because detectives advised not to pursue the vehicle if it didn't stop. I watched as the suspect tried to pass the other vehicle while it was making a left turn, causing a crash. I notified other units over the radio and pulled up to the crash. The driver of the suspect vehicle immediately jumped out of the driver's seat and ran. I detained the suspect's passenger and started checking on the other vehicle's occupants. I observed the suspect driver running from Officer D. The suspect jumped over a six foot wooden privacy fence and kind of smiled back, when on top of the fence, thinking Officer D wouldn't be able to follow. Officer D was running at a good pace, lowered his right shoulder into the privacy fence breaking a four by four post, and two entire sections of that fence were knocked to the ground. About one minute later, Officer D brought the handcuffed suspect from the rear yard.

***

A call came into the communications center from a mother that was having problems with her son. The mother had to walk up to the corner store to make the call, because she did not have a phone at the residence. The mother advised that her son was a 40 year old black male, and he had active arrest warrants. I was able to confirm, while in route, that the son had an active arrest warrant for a violation of probation on a possession of cocaine charge.

I responded to the call and arrived as the mother was making her way back to the residence. The mother walked up to the front door with me and advised that her son was just inside the door watching television.

The mother added that her son did not have a job and would not let her watch the television channel that she wanted to watch. I walked into the residence and observed the 40 year old black male sitting on the couch watching television. I handcuffed the suspect and started to take him outside to my cruiser. The black male advised that he did not want to go to jail wearing the slippers that he had on his feet and asked if he could get some different shoes. The suspect was still handcuffed behind his back, when I led him down a short hallway to his bedroom.

The suspect's bedroom was only about nine feet by eight feet wide and had a single bed, a chest of drawers, and a tiny night stand. The suspect pointed to the pair of shoes on the floor that he wanted to wear. I observed three to four crack cocaine pipes laying in plain view between the suspects chest and night stand. I took possession of the crack cocaine pipes and advised the suspect that he was also going to be charged with possession of cocaine.

Approximately six months later, I had a hearing of a motion to suppress evidence. The defense was attempting to have the court not allow the submission of the crack cocaine pipes as evidence. These motions are almost always full of incorrect information about the officer's actions and claim that the defendant's constitutional rights were violated in some way. When the defendant walked into the courtroom, the judge stated, "Well, welcome Mr. S, you look good. It's amazing how getting off cocaine and eating three meals a day can improve your health." It is probably never a good thing for a defendant to be well known to the judge.

I testified in the motion to suppress and the judge denied the defenses' motion, so the crack cocaine pipes would remain as evidence. The probation officer testified that the defendant had failed required drug

tests while on probation, whic
of probation to the judge. The
attorney and the defendant th
sentence him under the violati
pled guilty to the cocaine offen
months concurrently. The defe
did not want to plead guilty to
The judge advised that if he we:
he could be sentenced to 72 mc
sentencing guidelines. The defe_____ advised that he
wanted to take the cocaine offense to trial, so the judge
advised, "Let's go to trial right now."

I testified once again with the same short story that I
just told, and I was obviously the only witness called for
the trial. After my testimony, the defense advised that
they did not have any witnesses to testify and almost
threw up their hands in disbelief in the defendant's
ignorance. There were no closing statements from
either the prosecution or the defense. The judge
advised, "Ok, I hold the defendant guilty of possession
of cocaine and sentence you to 72 months. Not even
fifteen minutes had passed and the defendant just lost
another 36 months of freedom. Making bad decisions is
probably another side effect of smoking crack cocaine.

***

I scheduled myself to have Lasik eye surgery on a
Friday, and came back to work on a Monday. During
that Monday evening's shift, I went to a two story
apartment house that was divided into fifteen, one room
units. I stopped a subject on the property that did not
live at the residence and checked him for warrants. The
subject was a 35 year old black male and he had an
active arrest warrant for possession of crack cocaine. I
placed the suspect under arrest and upon a search
incident to arrest, I found him to be in possession of
crack cocaine. The suspect was charged with the
possession of cocaine and also arrested for the warrant.

...spect to the alley where my cruiser ...d asked him to have a seat in the rear. ...int, the suspect had been cooperative, but ...d to sit into the vehicle. I was able to talk him ...ting on the seat, but he still refused to pull his ...nto the cruiser. There was a small crowd that ...arted to gather along the edge of the alley that started to encourage his behavior. Officer R was my back-up unit and he had gone to the opposite side of the cruiser and started to pull the suspect into the vehicle, but the suspect hooked his feet under the bottom edge of the opened cruiser door.

At this point, Officer R and I had enough of his resistance and the heckling crowd was starting to become more vocal. Officer R pulled out his pepper spray and was about to spray the suspect in the face. I stopped Officer R because I wasn't certain what effect the residual spray would have had on my eyes from the recent surgery. I pulled out my ASP, extended it, and applied two strong strikes to the suspect's legs. I have never seen a pair of legs pulled into a vehicle as quick as the suspect responded. The heckling crowd also received the message loud and clear and walked off into their apartments.

Chapter 10

At the start of my third year, I put an application in to transfer to a Community Police Officer (CPO) position. CPO's are an extension of the patrol division and usually work in uniform. CPO's are assigned a specific area and their focus is on solving the long-term problems of that specific area. There are several police theories for accomplishing this problem solving, like the "SARA" method or "displacement" of crime, but common sense usually works too. CPO's usually were not directed by the communications center very much or by calls that came in through 911 and were free to work on making improvements to the assigned area.

Initially, when I submitted my application, Sergeant R gave my application back and advised me that I needed to have "two years off of probation" to apply. This department requirement meant that I would have had to wait another year. Three weeks later, Sergeant R called me at home on a Thursday and asked if I still wanted to be a CPO. I advised, "Yes, Sir", and Sergeant R replied, "Great, you will come to work on Monday as 714 (my new call sign)". I already had a reputation as a good police officer with a great work ethic, so there was no need for me to sit for some silly interview.

My newly assigned area was actually the same specific zone within the district that I was assigned in patrol on evening shift, so I was already familiar with the area. The area was seven by nine blocks of the inner-city with plenty of every crime category imaginable to work. I took the new positon very seriously and tried to identify what I could do to make improvements. The area was almost equally divided into two specific named neighborhoods with a busy avenue dividing them. One benefit of the CPO unit was you made your own work hours, or you could come in and work whatever schedule you wanted. In theory, this is so CPO's could work when they are having problems, but with an inner-city zone that meant any time of day. My schedule didn't change too much, because I preferred the evening shift and so did most criminals.

I worked on many problems simultaneously, but one of the first major problems that I identified within the zone was vacant and abandoned houses. These structures can be attractive nuisances to a great number of criminal offenses. I constructed a list of 85 vacant and abandoned residences and noted a great number of them that were not secure. I noted many of them that appeared to be active with having transients, prostitutes, or drug addicts using them. I started to secure these residences using the City's boarding agent. This is an individual that started a company securing residences after a crime, a breach for a search warrant, or where there was a structure not safe to leave accessible to others. I had the agent board up approximately 12 houses that were causing the majority of the problems in the area and almost over-night, many of the transients, prostitutes, and drug addicts were gone.

However, instead of getting a "great job", I received a memo from Fiscal Services in the police department. The memo advised that in the future I needed to make boarding requests through the City's Code Enforcement, which takes about six months to get a structure boarded if it ever happened at all. Fiscal Services advised that I single handedly spent the remainder of that year's police budget for boarding. My problems were solved and it really didn't matter to me what pocket, or City budget, the money came from.

My next project was identifying and removing all of the vacant and abandoned vehicles. If the vehicles were either parked on the road or in the alleyway there was a process for getting them removed. Once a vehicle was cited, or tagged, by the police department, it could be impounded if the owner did not move the vehicle within

72 hours. I impounded a great number of vehicles. There were also many inoperable vehicles that were on the private property of residences. I spoke with many residents about options for removing these vehicle and many complied. The remainder of inoperable vehicles, that were "eyesores" to the neighborhood, I turned over to the City Code Enforcement.

I also made a list of all of the non-residential or commercial entities within my zone. These could be described as businesses, churches, schools, etc. Even though the area was only seven by nine blocks, it included a variety of these entities. There were two schools, a post office, two funeral homes, a gas station, a Walgreens, and many other small businesses. I even had the local or "national" headquarters for the Uhuru Movement. This group could be described as a radical political organization promoting the economic and political freedoms of "black Africans". I preferred to call them American's. I personally went to each and every entity to introduce myself and inquire about any known criminal problems. I also worked closely with the two named neighborhoods within the zone. I made certain to emphasize to everyone that I contacted that my job was to deal with crime and I was not the new point of contact for all of the City's services.

As a CPO you were also expected to monitor every call that occurred within your zone and identify any crime patterns that developed. An example, of a crime pattern, would be a series of burglaries with similar methods to commit the offense. I used to always joke that the only crime pattern that I dealt with in my zone was "senseless violence". In reality, like many other inner-city zones, I also had on-going narcotic offenses.

The Community Policing Unit also worked many operations that addressed specific categories of crime, such as narcotic operations, prostitution operations, open container of alcohol operations, etc. Since these operations would benefit more than one specific zone, all of the CPO's from the district would work these together. The operations would also provide safety in numbers for officers and a chance to work as a team. I made a point to assist in operations in all three districts of the City. The Community Policing Unit was a perfect position for a self-motivated officer, but it needed good supervisors to monitor the CPO's that were not self-motivated.

***

We had a prostitution operation scheduled for one day from 0600 hours to 1400 hours. I had planned to leave for vacation later that same day, so I thought that the schedule would work perfect for me. First thing in the morning, Officer A and I were loading all of the required equipment into the rear of an SUV at the rear of the station. There was one piece that was a large suitcase that contained the recording device that weighed about fifty pounds and was bulky. The piece was too heavy for Officer A to pick-up and place into the truck, so she devised another method. Officer A picked the suitcase up holding it at her hip and swung the unit around by twisting her body and utilizing her right leg to hoist the suitcase into the rear of the SUV.

This plan may have worked, but I was bending over at the time picking up some duffle bags. As I bent over the suitcase was being swung around and it struck me in the center of the top of my forehead. The blow knocked me backward about five feet and caused me to "see stars". Like any head wound, the blood poured. I went to the emergency room and received about ten stitches. I spent the remainder of that shift and my entire vacation with a large bandage on my head.

***

One evening, I initiated a traffic stop on a vehicle for an improper tag, which was later determined to be a stolen tag. The black male, suspect driver of the vehicle initially attempted to pull quickly into a driveway to avoid the traffic stop. As the suspect pulled into the drive, he struck a small concrete block wall that ran along the edge of the drive. As I approached the vehicle on foot, the suspect jumped out of the vehicle and started looking in both directions for a place to run. I quickly grabbed the back of the suspect's clothing and asked if he had a driver's license. The suspect initially stated, "No" and then quickly stated, "Yes." Next, the suspect advised that his license was inside the residence that he had stopped at.

I advised the suspect that I would confirm his license status from the computer in my cruiser and called for a back-up unit to assist me. I walked the suspect over to my cruiser and he started bracing and pushing backward against my efforts to walk. I advised the suspect that he was being detained and that he needed to have a seat in the rear of my cruiser. I patted the suspect down in the rear doorway of the cruiser, to ensure that he didn't have any weapons on his person. The suspect started to push backward toward me several times, but I had a hold of his shirt. I pushed the suspect against the rear quarter panel of the cruiser causing it to dent. Next, the suspect partially turned toward me and pushed me backward with his hand.

I advised the suspect that he was under arrest and that he needed to put his hands behind his back. I made the mistake of releasing my grip on the suspect's pants to take him to the ground utilizing an arm bar take-down. The suspect twisted away from me and pushed the center of my chest causing me to come down on my left hip and the back of my head struck the asphalt. On my way to the ground, I was able to grab ahold of the suspect's shirt, but I was now on my back. The suspect also grabbed his own shirt yanked up on it and then down quickly slamming the back of my head against the asphalt again. Everything went black for a

81

brief moment and then I realized that I still had a grip on the shirt. I yanked the shirt toward me and the suspect pushed off of my chest with both hands and slipped out of his shirt.

I advised over the radio that I was now in foot pursuit of the suspect, that I had battery on law enforcement charges, and that I needed a K-9 unit to respond. I called for units to set a perimeter. The suspect ran into the rear yard of a corner house through an open gate on a privacy fence. On the other side of the yard, the skinny suspect slipped through a hole in the fence where two slats were missing. I ran to the fence and kicked a few more slats off, making an opening big enough for myself and continued running after the suspect.

I lost sight of the suspect when he ran around a residence on the next street. Back-up units had taken perimeter points and the K-9 began to track for the suspect. About twenty minutes later, the suspect tried to run from the K-9 dog when he was located. The K-9 bit the suspect in the leg and in the scrotum. I can't say I was sorry to hear that. The suspect ended up with numerous charges for his actions and also had a container of crack cocaine in his vehicle that was located in the search. The suspect ended up being sentenced to three years in prison.

***

I observed a gold Jeep Wrangler circling in a known drug sales area just outside my zone. I conducted a traffic stop of the vehicle due to it having an expired tag and a cracked windshield. I had to confirm the driver's license status in the computer, because the white male driver did not have his license in his possession. I wrote the driver a citation for the expired tag and after that asked the driver if I could search his vehicle. The driver stated that he did not want me to search his vehicle and admitted to "dabbling in the stuff" when I asked about narcotics.

I left and made an unrelated traffic arrest for driving on a suspended license and then observed the white male suspect with the gold Jeep a second time. It had been 45 minutes since my first encounter with him and this time he was in my zone. The white male had parked his Jeep along the curb at a stop sign and was walking back to it from a known drug sales house. I stopped my cruiser and started walking up toward the white male on foot. As I approached, the suspect touched the hood latch of the Jeep acting as if he was fixing something. The suspect then turned, walked toward me, and stated, "Man if you are looking at the Jeep, I just got a ticket for it; Officer Bizzell gave me a ticket for the tag and he is kind of a friend of mine."

I almost laughed out loud at his statements and then I believe the suspect recognized me from 45 minutes earlier. The suspect started making spontaneous statements about "jonesing" for narcotics and "I just came down here to buy a crack rock, but I don't have any money". I asked the suspect if he was able to find a crack rock, and if I could search his person. The suspect consented to a search and I located a burnt piece of wire brillo pad used for smoking crack cocaine. I advised the suspect that he was under arrest and he stated, "Man I forgot I had that in my pocket." I also located a single crack rock at the suspect's feet on the sidewalk.

Once in handcuffs and in the back seat of my cruiser, the suspect told me that he used to have a "six-figure job" and now all he owned was his Jeep and a couch in his apartment. I informed the suspect that I had some bad news for him, because now all he owned was a couch. I seized the Jeep through the State of Florida Asset and Forfeiture Act and took the suspect to jail.

***

I was dispatched to a call of a man with a gun. An
anonymous citizen told an off-duty unit that there was a
suspect with a gun in his pants pocket and gave a full
description of the suspect. Upon arrival, I observed the
suspect as described, a black male wearing a light green
jacket and white shorts, sitting on a wall by a
convenience store. I advised my back-up unit that I
would approach from the north and that he should hold
to the south.

Upon the sight of our cruisers, the suspect initially
attempted to walk away to the south and then started
running. The suspect was caught by us just prior to
jumping over a chain link fence at a residence. After the
suspect was handcuffed, we located a chrome .38
caliber semi-automatic handgun in his rear pocket. The
suspect was charged with carrying a concealed firearm,
which carried a minimum mandatory sentence of three
years in prison.

***

I was working a narcotics operation with other CPO's
that was being supervised by Sergeant S. A couple
hours into the shift, Sergeant S called for some back up
units. He advised over the radio that a suspect had run
from him and had just run into a small convenience
store in the neighborhood. I responded and found
Sergeant S standing in the doorway of the store and
observed the suspect standing in one of the isles not
knowing which way to run. I entered the store with
another CPO and placed the suspect under arrest with
minimal resistance. We located crack cocaine and
marijuana on the store shelves that the suspect
attempted to hide in front of officers.

The defense attorney's on the case filed a motion to
suppress the evidence, so Sergeant S and I were
subpoenaed to court. We both testified and then
returned to the courtroom to hear the judge's verdict on

84

the motion. The judge granted the motion, which meant the narcotic evidence would not be allowed in court. The judge described why he felt that Sergeant S had improperly detained the suspect, via the store, prior to the arrest.

Sergeant S had decided that he had heard enough, stood up and left the courtroom abruptly while the judge was still speaking. As Sergeant S left he pushed hard on the bar to open the exit door, which made a loud noise. I had no intention of following Sergeant S out of the courtroom and sat quietly listening to the judge although I also disagreed with the ruling on the abandoned narcotics.

After the motion ended, the judge called the Assistant State Attorney up to the front of the courtroom and started to advise him that he wanted him to get with Sergeant S and lecture him on his behavior in court. After getting the judge's instructions, the Assistant State Attorney quickly turned to me to pass that responsibility of relaying that message on to me. I responded back to the station and just prior to my arrival, I asked Sergeant S to meet me in the lobby of the station. I had not noticed, but Sergeant D had just checked out at the lobby of the station prior to my request.

Sergeant S arrived in the lobby and I passed on the judge's message to him. Sergeant S looked relieved and stated, "That's it, I thought you were calling me down to the lobby with Sergeant D to arrest me for contempt of court." We both laughed it off and went out to lunch.

Chapter 11

Part of a CPO's responsibility is to get to know the residents of the area or zone that he works. I became very aware of people's habits within the zone, as well as who lived in the neighborhood and who didn't. I was aware of what vehicles were normally in the zone and knew many of the problem residents. I made a point to periodically check a long list of these subjects for active warrants, valid driver's licenses, and verified that vehicles had valid tags. I even had a binder full of residents within the zone and the surrounding area that I dealt with on an ongoing basis.

***

One evening, I was working a special narcotic operation in an unmarked vehicle with Detective E riding with me. I observed a 1984 gold Oldsmobile Cutlass Supreme that was known to me by a resident in my zone and known to have an improper tag. The driver was a known subject that lived at a known narcotic sales house. I called for marked cruises to come and stop the vehicle. The suspect initially stopped for two marked cruisers, but then drove off westbound. The suspect was only about three blocks from his residence, so I assumed he was fleeing there. I responded to that location and watched the suspect park at the residence and then run off in a northeast direction. I instructed units where to go to locate the suspect and we arrested him without further incident.

I had recently recovered a vehicle of the same year that had been stolen from a different jurisdiction that had the motor stolen out of it. The suspect admitted that he did not know if the motor in his vehicle would come back as stolen. Since the vehicle was used in the commission of a felony, the fleeing and eluding, we seized the vehicle under the State of Florida Asset and Forfeiture Act. The information was forwarded to the auto theft detectives for them to try to identify the serial numbers. The suspect was transported to jail.

***

I was working with the narcotic units to help identify subjects in a buy bust operation. One of the undercover detectives had made a purchase of crack cocaine, but had lost sight of the suspect before he was identified. Sometimes I could make the identity within my zone without even having to stop and get out with the suspects because it would be someone that was known to me. The detectives advised that they lost the subject as he rode away on his red bike in a northeast direction. Then Detective D provided a description of the suspect as a 20 year old black male, with platted hair, about 5 foot six, weighing 150 pounds, had a black wrap on his head, wearing blue jean shorts and a white tank top, and riding a red bike.

About two minutes later, I observed 20 year old black male, with platted hair, about 5 foot six, weighing 150 pounds, had a black wrap on his head, wearing blue jean shorts and a white tank top, and riding a red bike up into a yard two blocks to the northeast. I stopped my cruiser and checked out with the subject as he walked onto the front porch. I attempted to get a good identification on the subject, but I knew that he was lying to me about his name. Since I could not confirm who the subject was, the detective advised me to simply arrest him and he would talk to him at the rear of the station. The detective advised that as long as the suspect had a round circular scar on his right shoulder that the detective would not need to come and verify that it was the same individual that sold narcotics to him. I looked and the subject had a round scar on his right shoulder, so I arrested him and transported him to the station.

Detective D came out of the interview room with a surprised look on his face and told me that the subject that I arrested was not the same subject that had sold narcotics to him. We eventually figured out the subject's identity, and luckily he had an active arrest warrant.

***

While patrolling one evening shift within my zone, I ran the tag on a 1980 Oldsmobile Cutlass. The tag came back with a hit from NCIC/FCIC and was registered to a car lot. I initiated a traffic stop on the vehicle and it pulled into a driveway at a residence that was known for narcotic sales. There was a group of black males standing in the front yard that were all known by me.

I called for a back-up unit to assist me on the stop. After Officer S arrived on scene, I asked the driver to step out of the vehicle. When the driver stepped out of the driver's seat, I observed a four inch glass crack cocaine pipe located under his right leg. I placed the suspect under arrest for possession of crack cocaine. Upon a search incident to arrest, I located a single edge razor blade, a small baggie of marijuana, and a cardboard cutout of a gun covered in a black nylon sock. I also located three blank checks belonging to a local grocery store that were probably taken in a burglary. Next, I located a driver's license, credit card, and social security card belonging to a victim of an armed robbery on the previous evening.

I remembered viewing a surveillance video from a robbery to a Chevron gas station in read-off approximately one week prior to that date. The video was kind of humorous because the clerk pretended that he could not open the register and the suspect (my suspect driver) tried to take the entire register. The video showed that the robbery suspect could not get the register because it was plugged in and the cord kept pulling him backward. The video suspect not only looked just like my suspect, but he also had a signature gray spot in the front of his hair about the size of a quarter.

I had the car lot owner respond to recover his vehicle and transported the suspect to the station for interviews with robbery detectives.

*****

We were commonly dispatched to a regional trauma hospital that was within the district to take reports on victims being treated there. One evening, I was dispatched to a "victim" with an unusual injury. The victim had a laceration to the skin around the base of his penis. The call taker advised that the cutting occurred in another part of the City.

I interviewed the victim as he laid in the surgery bed being prepped for surgery. I observed the cut to be on the top side of the penis and started at the scrotum on one side and ended at the scrotum on the opposite side. The doctor advised that only the skin was cut and a small artery on the right side of the penis. The victim had an oxygen mask covering his mouth and appeared to be under the influence of some type of narcotic. The victim gave several conflicting stories about how the cutting occurred and was trying to blame another male in his apartment building. I documented all of the versions of the "truth" in my report. When the control officer arrived, I responded to the "crime scene" to attempt to speak with any witnesses, but no one knew anything.

*****

We were working an auto theft detail within the district with all of the CPO's. I was working in plainclothes and driving an unmarked rental vehicle with Officer M riding with me. Our job was to locate, follow, and recover as many stolen vehicles as we could. We were driving down an avenue, when a 39 year old black male yells, "Twenty piece man?" He assumed that we were in that area to purchase crack cocaine. As we

90

continued driving, the suspect was following our vehicle down the center of the avenue.

I called for uniformed units to respond and check out with the suspect. We responded back to the scene, as soon as officers stopped the suspect. Officer M located what would have been considered a half piece of what we initially believed to be crack cocaine. We located a full sized piece at the suspect's feet. The suspect initially denied trying to do anything or to selling narcotics. Finally, the suspect admitted, "Oh, that's just slap", meaning that the substance that we had located was fake crack cocaine. The suspect admitted that he was trying to sell the fake substance to "stupid white guys". The suspect advised that he was a crack cocaine addict and was trying to make some money, so he could buy some real crack cocaine. The suspect was arrested and charged with selling fraudulent narcotics. Yes, there is a law for that offense.

***

Another operation that I was assigned to as a CPO, was working roadside vending. We were asked to organize an operation to combat all of the curbside food sales or sales from food trucks. For someone to open a brick and mortar restaurant, they have to cut through a lot of governmental red tape. Normally, to cut that tape takes a great deal of money or many application fees. Once they have a legitimate restaurant operational, the last thing an owner wants is for someone to drive up in a food truck and feed all of their potential customers. There are certain licenses that traveling food trucks could obtain with restrictions on where they sell their products. There isn't any license obtainable to someone to pull out a bar-b-que grill and start selling chicken on the street corner.

We were working with supervisors and agents from the State of Florida Division of Food Safety. The City and the police department always preferred to start out with an "education phase" on any new operations that we worked. We were instructed to locate the roadside vending locations and the state agents would respond to educate the violators. Sometimes this approach backfires, because when someone is not "cited" or arrested they assume that the police are just messing with them. Most of the individuals that we spoke with became irrational and upset, like we were in the wrong and taking money out of their pockets.

***

We were advised by supervisors that they wanted the CPO's to address the problem of sales of pirated CD's on the roadside. We were advised again to "educate" individuals prior to taking any enforcement. I was lucky because I only had one location, where an individual was setting up a tent to sell pirated CD's.

I stopped and spoke to the suspect, who was a 25 year old black male. The suspect advised that he had two other black males that worked for him and that they had been selling CD's there for months. He didn't think I was being fair because there were many places around the area that other individuals were selling CD's. I continued to "educate" him that he was breaking the law and violating numerous copyright infringements.

The suspects set up their booth again the next day and I had to respond to the location to "educate" them again on the laws. I learned from our Intelligence Unit that to verify the copyright violations each CD had to be analyzed by the record company's regional representative and they do not do that too often.

A couple days later, I again observed the CD's being sold from the same booth at the same location. I stopped and issued the suspect a criminal violation with a court date for the following month. As "evidence" of the crime that was continually being committed, I seized everything. I loaded my cruiser up with over 500 CD's, chairs, tables, two portable CD players, and a large portable tent. I am quite certain the evidence clerks cursed me that day.

***

I was very used to clearing out or ensuring that the vacant and abandoned houses within my zone stayed vacant. Allowing even one transient to set up his "home" there was not only inviting things like narcotics and prostitution, but it was also inviting other crimes like burglaries and robberies. The majority of crack addicts do not work and they get their money through other means to support their habit. I had contacted the owners of some of the vacant properties and had permission to arrest anyone that was even trespassing. Other structures were truly abandoned with owners that lived in other states. I even had one large structure where the elderly owner lived in Spain.

Usually, I would try to get a back-up officer if I was going to search the structures for problems. Sometimes if it was daytime and the District was busy, I would simply do it by myself. Even in the daylight, some of the structures were pitch black inside with all of the windows boarded shut.

One day, I was working a dayshift and driving through the alleys. I came upon a residence that had been fully boarded for years. On this day, I observed the plywood that had covered the rear door was pulled away leaving the doorway wide open. I called for a back-up unit to respond to assist me, but the dispatcher advised that no one was available. This was an all too common problem throughout my career. I decided to investigate the residence a little further on my own. As soon as I entered through the doorway, I could smell an unusual burning smell that I assumed was crack cocaine. I had arrested plenty of people with crack cocaine rocks, pipes, and other narcotic paraphernalia, but had never actually been exposed to the smell of crack cocaine burning. I was quite confident that someone was inside the residence, so I announced my presence and commanded anyone inside to identify themselves.

The doorway was the only opening that was allowing light to enter the structure and it was on the east side. I could only see about ten feet past the entry room due to a closed door and a pile of furniture. I walked about eight feet away from the doorway into a room to the north and shut off my flashlight to wait and listen for any noises. After approximately 90 seconds, I heard the sound of someone running on the floor toward the only open door. I had my flashlight in my left hand and my issued Glock semi-automatic handgun in my right.

I moved quickly toward the doorway to block the suspect's path. I grabbed ahold of the front of the suspect's shirt, while still maintaining a grip on my flashlight. I had my firearm very close to my right chest to ensure that the suspect did not grab at it. I pushed the suspect up against the wall to the left of the entry door and observed Suspect L, a subject known to me. I pulled Suspect L outside of the structure holstered my firearm, and handcuffed him. I yelled at Suspect L telling him that I almost shot him. Suspect L was a 37 year old black male crack addict that lived two houses away with his mother.

I notified the dispatcher that I had arrested someone, and again requested a back-up unit. Officer C arrived and I had him stand by with Suspect L, as I searched the remainder of the structure. No one else was inside, but I did recover a glass crack pipe and a bottle of old prescription pills. I questioned Suspect L, but he never would admit to smoking crack in the structure or possessing the pipe. I ended up charging Suspect L with loitering and prowling and transported him to the jail.

***

Many private businesses want to "hire" police officers to protect their employees, customers, and assets of the business. The police department would contract all of these jobs with businesses and then assign officers on a rotational schedule to the jobs. Police officers call this "off-duty work", or "off-duty assignments". Examples of some of the assignments are working at a bank, movie theater, church traffic, and countless bar jobs. Some off-duty work is city sponsored events like parades, park festivals, etc. I worked my share of off-duty assignments.

One evening I was working one of the bar jobs, which were normally Friday and Saturday nights from 2300 to 0200 hours. I was working at a bar that most officers tried to avoid due to its' location. The bar was known for having many "thugs" hanging out. I knew a lot of subjects and always kept an eye out for individuals that were wanted. Approximately two weeks prior to this assignment, I had a suspect that fled from me in a traffic stop driving a 1995 green Geo Tracker. I watched as the same vehicle pulled past the front of the bar. The vehicle stopped briefly, due to traffic, and I was able to confirm that the driver was positively the same suspect from my fleeing and eluding offense. I watched as the suspect parked his vehicle and walked into the bar with his girlfriend.

I was working the assignment with Officer C and I called for a couple more units to respond to assist with the arrest and the crowd after the bar closed. Of course, the suspect stayed until closing time, 0145 hours, and a large crowd emptied from the bar. I approached the suspect with other officers and placed him into handcuffs with minimal resistance. Once I started walking the suspect to my cruiser, he became enraged. Part of the suspect's rage was playing it up for the crowd, because he didn't want my arrest to impact his image. The suspect was screaming racially charged statements referring to us as "crackers", making threats, and screaming "fuck you" as loud and as often as a person could. Once inside my cruiser, the suspect initially tried to kick out the left side rear glass window.

I drove the suspect to the rear of the police station, which was only ten blocks away. After a couple of minutes, the suspect apologized to me for the way that he acted. I don't know if the suspect ever knew, but I had assisted in arresting him a few years earlier after he fled from Officer H on a traffic stop.

About three years later, the suspect was wanted again for violent felonies and was observed by myself and other undercover detectives in the area of that same bar. The suspect fled again from a marked police cruiser and a pursuit was initiated. The suspect drove the wrong way on the interstate, so the pursuit was cancelled. The suspect ended up continuing in the wrong direction and running head on into a vehicle on the interstate and killing the innocent driver. The suspect was later convicted for that offense.

Chapter 12

As a CPO, I could work basically any schedule that I wanted. Our chain of command preferred that we spread our hours over five days. I believe that this preference was to have CPO's available to the staff, if needed, and also so patrol officers didn't become too jealous of our flexible positions. I usually worked four long days and then one shorter one, with plenty of off-duty work surrounding those hours. Patrol officers at the time were all assigned eight hours shifts with a rotating schedule for their off days. Patrol officers did not have any flexibility in their schedules and usually did not have a choice on the calls that they were dispatched to work. Patrol officers were directed by the number of calls that came in through "911" or directly into the communications center, and many days patrol officers did not even get lunch.

I was one of the CPO's that made a point to take dispatched calls for patrol officers. I knew that our patrol division was working under staffed and that on many days patrol officers would even be denied vacation requests due to staffing levels. I looked at the schedules of a few of our neighboring agencies and found that a few of the patrol divisions worked ten hour shifts, a few worked twelve hour shifts, and one agency worked eleven hour shifts. The agency with the eleven hour shifts had an "A" and a "B" squad and had a perpetual four days on and four days off rotation. I knew that things could be better for our patrol officers.

In researching these schedules, I found that many agencies lowered mandatory overtime and improved officer moral by switching to a longer shift. Working the longer days resulted in a four day work week for officers with three days off every weekend. I compiled a packet of the research along with several models of the three districts of our patrol division working either a ten or twelve hour shift. I put it in an inter-company envelope and sent it to the Chief of Police with no name on it, because I didn't care who wanted to get credit for a positive change. In large organizations, sometimes there is resistance to any suggestions that come up from "the bottom".

A few weeks later, I heard that Sergeant R was looking into ten hour shifts for patrol and was forming a staffing committee. I met with Sergeant R to get on the committee and Sergeant R, Dispatcher T, and I worked on the project for a few weeks. In our first meeting, Sergeant R pulled out some of the paperwork that I had sent to the chief, which had a handwritten note that stated, "Gary, Please look into this and see what we could do. Lieutenant Z." I almost laughed out loud, but never told anyone. Based on our authorized staffing numbers and the reality of an actual strength number of our patrol division, we were only able to devise ten hour shifts for evening shift and mid-night shift. The staffing levels forced us to leave our dayshift working eight hour shifts, but many dayshift officers liked that fact anyway. A few months down the road the new patrol plan with ten hour shifts was implemented and it's the same schedule that patrol officers still work today.

***

I was riding as a two man unit with Officer L, another CPO. I heard a call dispatched of "check welfare" on an individual who missed a dialysis appointment and we were two blocks away. I advised Officer L that we should take care of it. Initially, Officer L put up some resistance because it would take hours if it was an unattended death and we were planning to eat lunch soon. I advised Officer L that if it was an unattended death, I would do everything and afterward buy him lunch. We advised the dispatcher over the radio that we would handle the dispatched call.

Upon arrival, there was no answer at the apartment door, so we located the on-site manager and luckily he had a key to the door. I will never forget the look on Officer L's face when the door was opened and the interior chain was still attached. We both pretty much knew that there was a deceased body inside. I had to remove a pin from the interior chain to gain access and we located the deceased inside. We called rescue to the scene to confirm the death and notified a sergeant of the circumstances. The deceased was a 51 year old Asian male and was lying beside his bed, face down, with his arms crossed beneath him and had no visible signs of trauma.

We located a phone number for the deceased's doctor and he was willing to sign the death certificate. The deceased had been in terrible health, as evidenced by the 15 different prescription medications found on scene and he had pictures from a recent colonoscopy. The Medical Examiner's Office was notified and they released the body to a removal service. We located a next-of-kin for the deceased in North Hills, CA and she was notified through their police agency. I don't remember where I bought lunch for Officer L.

***

I was dispatched to a call of an unattended death of a child. I was advised that rescue units were on scene and had pronounced the death and that the dispatcher would notify detectives at our department. The scene was inside a large apartment complex with two story buildings. All of the structures had exterior stairwells that lead to the second floor units. The deceased was inside one of the second floor, two bedroom apartments.

Upon arrival, I observed an already chaotic scene, with many residents out in the parking lot attempting to find out what was happening. I entered the apartment and spoke briefly with the rescue personnel to obtain their actions on their call as well as their identities. The complainants that had called "911" were the grandparents of the deceased and they were present inside the apartment. The deceased child was a 21 month old black male and was observed lain on his back on the living room floor beside a pool table. The child was only wearing a diaper and his arms were in a raised position with both fists clenched. Only slight rigor mortis had set in upon my arrival and the child did not have any sign of physical trauma.

Normally, the rescue personnel kind of hand over a death scene to the police and go back into service to handle other calls. On this day, none of the personnel were too quick to leave, due to being in the presence of a deceased child and the helpless feelings that come with that scene. I obtained the initial, brief statements from the grandparents separately. Both told the same basic story. The child's mother dropped the deceased off at approximately 1040 hours and went to work. After only a couple minutes, the child threw up some orange vomit, so they removed all of his clothing, cleaned him up, and laid him in the bed with a wet towel on his neck. The grandfather laid down with the child and fell asleep. The grandfather advised that when he woke after two hours, he could not wake up the child and he screamed for his wife. The grandmother advised that the child was cold, so she ran and called "911", as the grandfather brought the child to the living room. The grandmother advised that she attempted to perform CPR, but the child's jaw was stiff and his nose was stuffed up.

The child's father was a 20 year old black male and was in prison. The child's mother was an 18 year old black female. The mother had already been called at work to come home, due to something being wrong with her child. The mother had not been notified of the death. Prior to her arrival, three detectives from my agency had arrived on scene to take over the investigation into the death of the child. The mother arrived and was clearly in a state of panic, after seeing all of the activity. Detective B started into a long drawn out explanation of what the grandparents' actions were, the actions of rescue personnel, and what everyone was doing, but had yet to tell the mother that the child had died. I could see the mother's confusion and anxiety getting worse, wanting to know if her baby was alright. Finally, I looked the mother directly in the eyes and stated, "Ma'am, your baby passed away." The mother screamed and appeared like her knees started shaking. I took ahold of the mother and sat her down into a chair. A longer explanation was not going to stop any of the mother's grief.

Obviously, a mother's strongest natural instinct is to pick up a child and make everything better. The mother pleaded with detectives on scene to allow her to hold her child. One of the hardest things about a death scene is controlling the integrity of the scene with family members. Prior to the mother's arrival, rescue personnel had covered the child with a small, yellow, plastic blanket. Eventually, the mother was allowed to kneel beside her child, as we pulled back the plastic blanket, so she could kiss the child goodbye. The medical examiner's office personnel arrived and took custody of the body of the child.

***

I was working an off-duty job at a popular local bar, which was located inside a large entertainment complex. At this assignment, I stood outside the entry doors to the bar on a busy exterior, second floor walkway. From my positon, I could monitor some of the activity inside the loud, crowded bar and was easily accessible to the bar's security. I had worked so many bar jobs that I could tell early in the night subjects that would end up being a problem.

On this night, I observed a white male, who would later become Suspect C, with another white male enter the bar. I could tell that they each probably drank a six pack on the way to the bar. Approximately 45 minutes later, two security officers were walking Suspect C out toward me and Suspect C states, "I don't know what happened in there, I was just fighting." Suspect C asks me if he was cut anywhere and I did not observe anything. I escorted Suspect C downstairs while talking to him. Suspect C was acting like he was a victim the entire time and told me that he used to be an officer in a nearby jurisdiction. Suspect C admitted that he was fired for "roughing up a crack dealer".

I was working the bar with Officer G and he was investigating what transpired inside the bar. Officer G advised that he had a victim with lacerations and Suspect C was going to be the aggressor. I interviewed a few witnesses and the victim on the lower level. The victim was struck in the back of the head with a beer bottle by Suspect C. After that initial strike, the victim tackled Suspect C onto his back and then Suspect C used the broken glass long neck, bottle in his hand to cut or stab the victim several times. The victim received stitches in three different lacerations on his head, including one next to his left eye. Suspect C was arrested, charged with aggravated battery, and taken to jail. Suspect C started the fight because the victim bumped into him on the dance floor.

***

At the entertainment complex, I had another incident working at another bar. I was assigned off-duty at a neighboring bar that was across a second floor exterior walkway from the bar above. There were two officers working off-duty at each bar and I was working with Officer G. I could see from across the walkway that security had brought two couples out of the other bar and Officer D met them at the doorway. Officer D took a few large beer glasses from Suspect H that had been hidden within a stack of plastic souvenir cups and pointed for the group to leave. The group walks over to the entrance of the bar that I am working and the bar security advised that they were not allowed inside.

The entire group was heavily intoxicated, as evidenced by the stack of plastic souvenir cups. I informed the group that they were not allowed into the bar and that they needed to leave the property. Of course, one individual in the group, Suspect H, takes issue with my statement. Suspect H proceeds to tell me that he does not have to leave, that I can't tell him what to do, and he was not going anywhere. I informed Suspect H if he refused to leave the property, he was going to be arrested for trespass after warning. Suspect H then proceeds to walk into the bar and walk circles in the crowd. I stood talking with the remaining three instructing them that they needed to get Suspect H and leave the property.

Suspect H returns to our location and starts telling the group that they do not have to leave. I again instructed Suspect H that he needed to leave the property and then asked him if he was going to leave. Suspect H turned away from me and continued telling the rest of the group that we can't make them leave. I took control of Suspect H with both of his hands behind his back and informed him that he was under arrest. Suspect H bent forward at his waist to pull away from me and I felt the Suspect H's fiancé almost jump onto my back, attempting to pull me back by my shoulders from behind. Officer D quickly pulled the fiancé away from me. Officer G took ahold of Suspect H's left upper arm and I was starting to put handcuffs on Suspect H. Suspect H starts to try to turn towards me in an attempt to prevent handcuffing. I released my hold of the suspect's left hand, knowing that Officer G has that arm and started to take Suspect H down to the floor with his right arm. Suspect H continued to resist our efforts and lunged forward in his stance, like a runner coming out of a starting position.

We still had control of the suspect's arms and he lunged directly into the metal posts on the second floor railing. The impact caused a two inch laceration to the top of the suspect's forehead, plenty of blood, and also took all of the remaining fight out of the suspect. Suspect H was handcuffed and then treated by rescue units. Upon a search incident to arrest, I located a large martini glass stuck down the suspect's pants that he was trying to steal. I informed the fiancé that she could be charged with battery on a law enforcement officer for her attempt to pull me away from Suspect H, but I knew she wasn't the real problem.

I had to take Suspect H to the emergency room for treatment and then out to the jail. Suspect H told me that he was going to sue me for $30,000 and that I was going to pay for his wedding. Suspect H did in fact file a lawsuit against me and hired a private attorney for that and for fighting the criminal charge. After a couple years, he accepted a guilty plea in criminal court and I stopped hearing about the civil lawsuit. I never did get an invitation to the wedding.

Chapter 13

A police officer, no matter how prepared, is always at somewhat of a disadvantage. In most circumstances, the police get to react to the actions of a suspect. In fact, the Use of Force Matrix in the State of Florida uses the wording "Response to Resistance" to describe an officer's force against a suspect. The police officer is issued certain tools to not only protect himself, but to also protect citizens and affect arrests. There are several intermediary tools that an officer can use like "OC spray" (Oleoresin Capsicum) or commonly called pepper spray, a police baton, and a Taser weapon. These weapons would be used on the way, or prior to using deadly force against a suspect. Police officers will meet force with force and sometimes are compelled to jump directly to deadly force. If a suspect pulls a gun on a police officer, the suspect should expect to get shot by the officer, period!

Through training and experience an officer becomes very familiar with the tools at his disposal and can access them from his duty belt during a confrontation or even while physically fighting. During some of my training, Officer R taught me a valuable lesson. We were timed at how long it took to pull our issued handgun and fire with actually hitting on target. I learned that I could see a threat, pull my firearm, and hit the threat in .85 seconds, or less than one second. This was a reassuring thought when thinking about all of the potential dangers on the street.

A good police officer knows how to deescalate a situation. Officers should never act on emotion or frustration when using force toward a suspect. Just like an officer escalates up the use of force matrix to match force with force, an officer must be able to also deescalate the force once a threat has been removed. Recognizing that the threat has been eliminated in a confrontation will be different for every police officer and no one else can make that call for the officer that is fighting.

This requirement to deescalate in no way means that a police officer should use physical force gently or sparingly. If there is a need to kick, punch, or take a suspect to the ground a police officer should carry out that force like someone's life depends on it. Even professional fighters lose fights by underestimating their opponents. One strike from a suspect can turn the table in any confrontation and a gun is always present even if it is only the officer's gun. A police officer is never simply required to accept any physical abuse from a suspect, merely touching a police officer is a felony crime and a police officer never has an obligation to retreat from force.

There are many videos that emerge of officers using force against suspects. It is almost impossible to know all of the facts that an officer knows or experience the situation through the eyes of the officer, simply by watching the video or worse a portion of a video. Many people take time to analyze videos and advise what action an officer should have considered, not realizing that an officer makes his decisions sometimes in less than a second. The State knows that it needs officers to be proactive and to take action when a crime is committed. Therefore, police officers have certain immunities with their actions and the force that they utilize against a suspect who is resisting. As long as an officer does not act with great negligence or malice, they normally have immunity for their actions. The State realizes that it is better to have an officer act and risk some error than to have a police force that does not act at all. Unless you are actually in the fight, it is almost impossible for you to know what level is using too much force. I have told many critics, if they think they can do a better job, police departments are always taking applications and remind them that officers normally encounter citizens on the worst day of the citizen's life.

I have arrested thousands of suspects and there is almost always some level of resistance. I learned that the strongest muscle a police officer can flex is their tongue, but I also learned you can't rationalize with irrational people. I have broken more than one suspect's ribs and had to get numerous suspects "medically cleared" prior to taking them to jail. I can state with 100% certainly that every physical use of force that I used was required and justified. I never had a single use of force complaint. Almost every suspect I arrested actually thanked me for treating them the way I would have wanted to be treated, even when force was used. Empathy is a great characteristic for a police officer to practice.

One year, Major B met Detective T and I in the hallway of the station and stated, "Hey you two, do you know that you all are ranked number one and number two in the total use of force incidents on the entire department?" That fact wasn't something that was published or celebrated, and each and every incident of force that we both had used was documented and justified.

***

While patrolling one day, I observed a 1989 blue Jeep Cherokee with an inoperable light. I pulled behind the vehicle and it made a couple of quick turns as I called the tag over the radio to check for any B.O.L.O.'s. The dispatcher advised that there were not any hits from the tag. I observed the vehicle not make a complete stop at a stop sign and I decided to initiate a traffic stop on the vehicle. The driver accelerated the vehicle a little and pulled into a vacant lot off of the street.

Both the driver and the passenger jumped out of the vehicle and started walking back toward me. The black male driver screamed, "Why did you pull me, man?" I instructed both of them to have a seat back inside their vehicle. Initially, it appeared like they were going to comply. The driver walked toward the driver door, grabbed the handle, and then walked around the front of the vehicle. I had been walking just behind the driver and I grabbed the back of his belt. The black male passenger had already opened the passenger door and was starting to sit down back in the front passenger seat. I again instructed the driver that he needed to sit back inside his vehicle. I was able to get the driver to sit inside the vehicle as Officer R arrived on scene.

The driver advised that he did not have his license on his person and provided his identifying information and I obtained a license from the passenger. I ran their information on the computer and learned that the passenger had a warrant for his arrest. I called for an additional back up officer and Officer L arrived on scene. I had Officer L stand at the driver's door of the suspect vehicle as myself and Officer R placed the passenger into handcuffs and into my cruiser. I returned to the passenger side of the vehicle and began a search inside the vehicle. The driver, Suspect S, stated, "You can just come up in the vehicle and look like that and move my shirt all around and stuff." At that moment, I had picked up a white t-shirt that covered a large bag with 25 individual small zip lock baggies filled with marijuana.

I ran around to the driver's side of the suspect vehicle as Suspect S started getting out of the driver's seat. I instructed Suspect S to put his hands behind his back, but Suspect S pushed Officer L back with his right forearm and pushed me away with his left hand. Suspect S looked like a fullback charging through the defensive line. Suspect S was only 5 foot eight inches tall, but weighed 200 pounds and was muscular. I ran right behind Suspect S and grabbed him from behind, but he was pulling me down a couple steps on the sidewalk to the street. Officer R also grabbed onto the suspect and Suspect S was throwing his elbows behind him in an attempt to knock us off. I was struck a minimum of four times, with one of the strikes hitting me in the left eye. I lost my contact lens and later had a headache.

Officer L joined in the fight with spraying Suspect S in the face with "pepper spray" and I attempted a couple of leg sweeps with negative results, as we crossed the street. When we reached the opposite curb, I utilized the curb and a leg sweep to bring Suspect S to the ground. As soon as Suspect S hit the ground, he stated, "Okay", as if to give up. I quickly handcuffed Suspect S behind his back. An officer should never assume that any suspect is done fighting. I advised over the radio that additional units could slow down their response and that we had handcuffed the suspect. Suspect S was placed into the rear of another marked cruiser.

I returned to the vehicle and found what the suspect was running from. There was a big crack cocaine cookie, a trafficking amount of cocaine, in the center console of the vehicle. Since the suspect made no admission to the cocaine and the vehicle was not registered to Suspect S, I knew the State Attorney's office may not file the charge. I had the clear baggie of the crack cocaine dusted for a fingerprint and the technician was able to lift one single print. I attended the State Attorney's investigation, where they decide if a charge will be filed. Attorney B informed me that he would not file the charge due to the reasons I already mentioned, but we did not have the results from the print. I walked over to the fingerprint technician's office and learned that the print did in fact come back to the right thumbprint of Suspect S.

I came back to Attorney B and advised him of my great news on the print. Attorney B initially informed me that they may still not file the charge even with the suspect's print on the crack cocaine bag. Attorney B explained to me that there was case law in other cases that could prevent it. Attorney B attempted to provide the example of him sitting in a room with a table full of cocaine bags and if I were to walk in, pick up a bag, and say, "Wow you have a lot of cocaine". Attorney B asked if the police busted in the room should we both go to jail. I replied, "Absolutely! And it sounds like time for you to create some new case law." Attorney B filed the charge and the suspect was convicted and sentenced to prison.

***

I responded with other officers to a call of a just occurred vehicle burglary. We waited on a perimeter until the K-9 officer attempted to track the suspect. The K-9 officer advised for units on the perimeter to circulate to look for the suspect. I noticed as soon as an officer left his position, a black male ran across the street westbound. I moved to that area and observed the individual walking on the sidewalk. I pulled next to the individual and asked him if he minded speaking with me. The individual agreed, so I exited my vehicle and started to speak with him. I asked the individual what was causing a bulge from his pants pocket. The individual stated, "Just a knife", stuck his right hand into the pocket, and bladed his right side away from me. I immediately trapped his right hand into that pocket, so he could not come out with the knife. I had the individual remove his hand slowly and informed him that I was going to remove the knife from his pocket and the individual advised that he understood.

I had ahold and control of the individual's right arm as I started to reach into his pocket. The suspect pushed me backward with his right forearm and his left hand on my chest, but I maintained control of the suspect with his right arm. I pushed the suspect against my cruiser and instructed him to place his hands on the hood of my vehicle. The suspect became cooperative and I called for an additional unit. The suspect was handcuffed, searched, and placed into the rear of my cruiser. I located an M & M candy container with three crack rocks inside and a small crack pipe in his pockets.

The suspect refused to provide his name to me, so I had to take him to the jail for fingerprint identification. The deputies at the jail informed me of his true identity as well as the fact that the suspect had six alias names as well as a parole warrant in the State of Florida for resisting an officer with violence.

***

I was working an off-duty assignment at a bar in an entertainment complex in the downtown area of the City with Officer C. I watched as a white male, extremely intoxicated, came walking over to the bar we were working. The suspect walked right up to Officer C and was talking with him at an extremely close distance and I observed Officer C tell him twice not to stand so close to him. Next, the suspect walked up to me and started making statements that I could not even understand due to his intoxication. I advised the suspect that he needed to continue walking to another location. The suspect walked off and I observed him walk into two different people and then try to enter into the bar. The security employees of the bar informed him that he was too intoxicated and was not allowed into the bar.

I observed the suspect turn around and walk into another subject. I walked over to the suspect and advised him that he needed to leave the entertainment complex and the suspect initially refused. I informed the suspect that I was going to escort him off of the property and control of his left arm. The suspect began tensing and stated, "You better let the fuck go of me", as he tried to raise his arms above his head. Officer C took control of his right arm and we proceeded to walk the suspect down to the lower level. About two thirds of the way down the steps, the suspect began to push his body up against mine and I informed the suspect that he was now under arrest. The suspect continued attempting to fight with us down the remaining steps.

When we reached the last step, I executed a leg sweep on the suspect bringing him down hard onto the paver courtyard onto his chest. I was on top of the suspect's back and Officer C had part of his weight on the suspect. The suspect was extremely muscular and refused to bring his hands behind his back for handcuffing. The suspect kept trying to get up off the ground and at one point did a push-up with both of us on his back.

I had called for back-up over the radio and other units in the complex responded to assist. An unidentified man ran up and threw down his wallet with a badge and also grabbed ahold of the suspect. I had already sprayed the suspect with "pepper spray", but this had minimal effect. It ended up taking a total of five of us to gain control of the suspect and get him into handcuffs. We stood the suspect up and walked him out to a cruiser. The suspect spun his head around and spit toward me and part of his spit glanced off of my forehead. I pulled the bottom of the front of the suspect's shirt up and over the top of his head covering his face to prevent any more spitting. The suspect was finally "defeated" and left the bar with his belly sticking out and wearing handcuffs.

***

I was working a special operation with homicide detectives to identify subjects in a certain location. I responded to the east side of an apartment building at the request of a couple detectives. Upon arrival, I observed the detectives and a couple other uniformed officers around a black male subject. As I was stepping out of my cruiser, I observed the black male pull away from Officer O and started high stepping and swinging his arms as Officer L attempted to also maintain a hold on him. I ran up and grabbed on to the suspect's shirt. The suspect went toward the ground a couple of times, but kept pushing up with his hands and feet.

I grabbed my "pepper spray" and sprayed the suspect directly in the face. The suspect stated, "Okay" and dropped onto the ground. The suspect was handcuffed, searched, and placed into Officer O's cruiser. The suspect was found to be in possession of crack cocaine.

A few minutes after the struggle, I realized that I had injured my left wrist. I went the emergency room, where we were required to go for all injuries and was given the standard 800 milligrams Ibuprofen. I continued working for months with pain in the left wrist and went to three different orthopedic surgeons, one of them wanted to literally cut my ulna bone (forearm bone) in half and shorten it. I did not go back to that surgeon. I worked with a hard nylon cast on the wrist for about a year and the wrist still would not heal. About 18 months later, I had minor surgery to repair a torn ligament in the wrist.

***

During the time that I was working with the hard nylon cast, I ended up receiving another injury. I was working with another CPO, Officer L, and we were at a duplex apartment within my zone. We located a black male subject in the second floor rear apartment that was supposed to be vacant. I obtained the suspect's identification and checked him for warrants. I learned via the radio that the suspect did have an arrest warrant.

The suspect was approximately 36 years old and was retired from the military. As soon as we attempted to take control of the suspect, he started physically fighting with us. We fought all the way down the stairwell to a very small entry hallway prior to maintaining control of the suspect and getting him into handcuffs. Somewhere between the top and the bottom step, I twisted and banged my right knee because I had a large bruise and it hurt to walk on it.

I went to the emergency room later that shift and received some more 800 milligrams Ibuprofen. Eventually, I was sent to an orthopedic surgeon three months later. During these three months, I was working my regular shifts with the injured left wrist and the injured right knee. The surgeon received the results from an MRI and informed me that I had a bone bruise. The surgeon continued to tell me that I had basically been "walking around on a broken leg for three months" and that I needed to have surgery to repair the meniscus. I continued working on the street until they scheduled the surgery.

***

Officer S had been in the CPO unit longer than any other officer. Officer S was extremely politically savvy, not only within the department, but also on the street. Officer S had a way with words to explain things and not make his statements sound negative to citizens. I heard Officer S provide an explanation to parents about their juvenile child's behavior more than once. Officer S would ask mothers, "Do you remember when you were little that your parents would tell you not to hang out with the wrong crowd?" The mothers always replied, "Oh, Yes". Then Officer S would state, "Well, let me tell you something, your son is the wrong crowd."

Chapter 14

The Community Police Officer's unit was always the go-to place for manpower to work any operations, any crime patterns, or to make special requests. I would constantly get requests from detectives to attempt to locate suspects with active probable cause for their arrests. The CPO's worked special operations with literally every unit in the police department and some other City departments. The training division had been hiring a great number of officers due to retirements and officers simply resigning. I assisted the training division with many training classes like geographic orientation, role playing in scenarios, and simunition, or non-lethal ammunition training.

**

A few months after one of the new trainees started working as a solo officer, he called for a back-up unit to arrest a suspect that had just boarded a city bus. I responded to assist the new officer and while in route obtained a detailed description of the suspect. The officer advised that the suspect was a 35 year old black male, who was wearing a plaid outfit, and provided his physical description.

I arrived in the area and we initiated a traffic stop of the city bus. I boarded the bus in front of the new officer and located the black male by the description that he had given. I had the suspect stand up and took control of his hands behind his back, so the new officer could handcuff the suspect. The new officer reached toward the suspect and placed his handcuff onto my left wrist. It was hard for me not to laugh out loud, but I simply grabbed my own handcuffs and put them onto the suspect. Both the suspect and I left the bus wearing cuffs.

**

On another call, I was dispatched to assist a new officer on a domestic battery offense. We arrived at the location, which was an expensive condominium in a high rise building. We made our way to the victim's unit and separated the couple for questioning. The State of Florida had a preferred arrest policy in domestic battery offenses and so did the police department. This policy was due to the high probability for actual physical violence to escalate. People tend to become the most violent with the ones that they love. There had been cases where officers failed to arrest on probable cause for battery, leave, and the suspect later killed the victim.

The new officer took down the statements from each. Basically, the husband had become infuriated with the wife about something, so he pulled some of her hair out, slapped her in the arm with her hairbrush, and threw her on the floor. The female victim had the hair that was pulled out, a mark on her arm, and a broken brush as evidence of what had occurred. After the new officer, documented all of the suspect's denials he stated, "Alright, well you folks have a great night" and started walking to the door to leave.

I pulled the new officer to the side and explained to him that he was forgetting to arrest the suspect. I advised the suspect that he was under arrest and would be coming with us. The suspect was a cooperative 68 year old white male and he was placed into handcuffs and transported in the new officer's cruiser. About half-way to the jail, the new officer called his sergeant and asked what he should do if his suspect was pale, sweating, and complaining of chest pain. The sergeant had to call rescue to respond to treat the suspect.

***

One evening, I worked in a different district with their CPO squad for a prostitution detail. I was working in full uniform and driving a marked cruiser with Officer L riding with me. We were responsible for physically arresting and transporting suspects.

116

After we transported an arrested female to the prisoner transport van at the rear of the station, I keyed up my microphone on the radio and asked if we were going to break for lunch. There was no response in my ear and after a few seconds I turned to Officer L and stated, "Well, I guess no one is listening to their fucking radio." A minute later, I was informed that the microphone button on my radio had stayed on and my statement was broadcast over the channel for everyone to hear. We ended up going to lunch. Every officer reminded me of my error by making various statements like, "Hey, Biz could you pass the fucking salt, anyone seen that fucking waitress, and looks like it might fucking rain."

***

On another prostitution operation, I had placed a 35 year old black female under arrest for solicitation and possession of crack cocaine. The female had an approximate four inch glass crack cocaine pipe with burnt brillo pad and cocaine residue on the pipe. I was about three blocks from the station and the black female advised that she was having trouble breathing. I called over the radio for the dispatcher to have rescue meet me at the rear of the station.

Many prisoners thought that they would not have to go to jail if they had medical problems and several had escaped from hospitals when receiving treatment. I assumed that the female was faking her problem like many suspects before her. As I pulled onto the rear parking lot, the female moaned and slumped forward against the cage of the rear seat. I am still assuming that the suspect was faking, but knew that I needed to get out and check on her. I parked my vehicle and walked around to the rear to check on her status.

The female was not responsive to my grabbing onto her or calling her name, so I was going to try pulling her out of the cruiser. I assumed that if she were faking she

117

would catch herself as her body went toward the asphalt parking lot. I grabbed the female suspect under her arms and pulled her out toward the parking lot. The female's body flopped against the asphalt as I was still holding her under her arms. I laid the female flat and advised the dispatcher to have rescue "step it up" because my suspect was not breathing.

I took the center of my right palm and placed it on the center of the suspect's chest and pushed. The female produced a moaning sucking sound that I am pretty sure I had heard before in a horror movie. After her first breath, the female was able to continue to breath on her own. Rescue units arrived and transported the suspect to the hospital, where she was put on a respirator for three days. The female had a severe asthma attack. I changed the charges for the suspect to misdemeanor offenses and assigned her a court date in the future, so we wouldn't have to babysit her in the hospital. That's a hell of a way to get out of a felony charge.

***

There was a large duplex residence in my zone that had been vacant. I observed about five young, black males that started hanging out in the lower level. They started sitting in the front yard in lawn chairs and on milk crates and would listen to the radio turned up loud. The subjects were obtaining electricity from a residence next door through an orange extension cord. There was a great deal of vehicle traffic that would stop for a couple minutes and then leave, which was indicative of narcotic sales. I knew that the duplex was up for sale from the realtor's sign in the front yard. I called the realtor on the phone to get the owner's information to inquire about the occupants. I had to initially leave a detailed voicemail message for the realtor.

The realtor called me back in a panic and advised that the property was supposed to be vacant, that no one had a right to be on the property, and the realtor was working on setting a closing for the property. The realtor advised that the owner did not want anyone on the property and advised that I had the permission to trespass anyone that was on the property.

Well that was all I needed to hear to respond to the property and take action against a problem house that was potentially disturbing other residents. I arrived at the residence and no one was there. I unplugged the extension cord, gathered up all of the boxes and crates that the group used to sit around the residence and transported it all to a dumpster, problem solved! The next day, the realtor called me back and informed me that he was sorry and he thought I was talking about another listing of his in a whole other county. Oops, I never heard any complaints from my actions, and the group never did return to that location.

***

A few of the CPO's were asked to assist the narcotics unit with a search warrant to a house. Our responsibility was to maintain an outer perimeter and catch anyone running away from the property. Upon arrival, the narcotic detectives advised that suspects were jumping out of the east side of the residence. Officer M and I observed a black male leave the property and run eastbound. We initiated a foot pursuit and lost sight of the suspect in the rear yard of a two story residence with an external stairwell that led upstairs.

The suspect was located on top of the stairwell. Upon seeing the suspect, Officer M pointed his firearm at him and yelled, "Let me see your hands I will fucking kill you!" I handcuffed the suspect and walked him back to the narcotic detectives. I returned to assist Officer M in searching the rear yard for any evidence that the suspect would have disposed of prior to his arrest. As soon as I started looking, two females walked out of the lower unit and one stated, "You see, I heard someone say I will fucking kill you and I knew it was the police."

***

I was working on a Sunday morning and patrolling through the neighborhood that was very quiet. I observed a three or four year old black female child standing out in front of a residence in what appeared to be her Sunday church dress. I thought that she looked cute, so I waved to the little girl. The girl raised the back of her right hand and slowly extended her middle finger. I laughed in disbelief.

I stopped my cruiser, exited, and walked up toward the child. The girl had a panicked look on her face and I walked past her to knock on the front door. A black female answered the door and I assume that it was the child's mother. I told her what happened and the mother screamed, "No!" The mother proceeded to yell at the girl and ordered her into the house as I returned to my cruiser and left the area.

***

I was dispatched to a single car injury accident to a parking lot that was located under the interstate. The dispatcher advised that rescue units were already on scene. I thought that this was an unusual place to have an injury accident. Upon arrival to the scene, I observed a white Chrysler K car that had been driven by a very fat 50 year old black female. The female advised that she was the driver and proceeded to tell me what happened. She advised that she entered the interstate on a street to the east and I knew that she was talking about an interstate exit ramp. The driver continued and advised that she realized that she was going the wrong direction and she wanted to take the nearest "exit ramp". Apparently, if you are going the wrong direction on the interstate exit ramp the overpass looked like an exit.

The driver had driven off of the pavement while driving the wrong direction as she approached the overpass and her vehicle flew off of a high embankment that ran between the entrance overpass and the exit overpass. The vehicle had to have been flying at least 30 feet in the air to clear a six foot fence that ran perpendicular on the roadway below. The vehicle cleared the fence, crossed that roadway, and bounced up into a parking lot on the west side of the road. The female informed me that she was not injured because she had her two airbags with her and motioned to her large breasts.

***

A call came in as a home invasion and provided a description of the four suspects and their suspect vehicle. Another patrol officer located the vehicle driving away from the area and attempted stop the vehicle. There were four black male suspects in the vehicle. The vehicle would not stop and was fleeing from the officer, so a pursuit of the vehicle was authorized. There was a "General Order", or rule that stated only two cruisers could be involved in a pursuit. All of the other cruisers in the district would always move to the area of the pursuit in an attempt to assist in arresting the suspect(s).

I moved toward the pursuit and eventually became the second cruiser in the pursuit when another officer became too far behind. I was calling the directions of the pursuit as we drove through neighborhoods. It looked like the suspects were heading toward the southbound entrance ramp for the interstate, which would have led them out of the City. For some reason the suspect turned just prior to interstate, onto a street that ended into a waterfront condominium complex. When the suspect vehicle reached the end of that street, all four doors of the vehicle opened and the four black male suspects ran in between the condo buildings.

I jumped out of my cruiser and started a foot pursuit on the closest suspect that I observed. I was closer to the suspect than he realized, because he ran and tried to jump over a three foot railing to someone's rear patio. As he was jumping over, I jumped onto his back and we both came crashing onto the rear patio set and landed on top of the patio table. There was an elderly white couple that was sitting at their kitchen table just inside the sliding door and I will swear in my memory that I can see the old man starting to take a bite of a large cheeseburger. The couple is watching in disbelief as the scene of me arresting the suspect on their back patio table.

My left leg was still hanging slightly over the railing as I am trying to pull the suspect's hands behind his back. I feel some intense pressure on my left calf. My first thought was, was there another officer trying to help me and they are grabbing onto me instead of the suspect? I turned around to see the police K-9 dog locked onto my left calf. Almost immediately the K-9 handler pulled him off of me and I finished handcuffing the suspect. All four suspects were arrested, because they had no idea where they were and did not belong in that complex. That was dog bite number two if you are keeping score.

***

At the start of my sixth year, I was still working as a CPO and had been looking for a suspect with warrants for about four months. I had arrested the subject a couple of times in the past and he stayed with his mother at a residence within my zone. The suspect was Suspect G and he had warrants for auto theft and fleeing and eluding, because he had fled from another officer.

I was working an off-duty job at a bar on a Friday night with Officer B. We were standing just outside the roped line for the subjects entering the bar along the sidewalk. I looked up and observed Suspect G about ten feet away, walking toward us into the roped line. I casually turned away from Suspect G and continued talking with Officer B, but did not have the ability to give Officer B too much warning for the arrest of Suspect G. As soon as Suspect G's back was toward us, I tapped Officer B on the arm and grabbed Suspect G from behind and the fight was on. Suspect G started spinning, pushing, and bending his body to break free from my hold. I was pulled into the rope line and poles and we both started to go toward the ground, but Suspect G broke free at the last second and pulled himself to his feet.

Next, Officer B grabbed onto Suspect G by his shirt and I observed Suspect G punch Officer B twice in the left temple as I was coming to my feet. Just as Suspect G was breaking free from Officer B I grabbed ahold of him and took him down to the concrete sidewalk. I was still struggling to keep Suspect G on the ground and Officer B started calling for back-up units. The bouncer from the bar came over and assisted in keeping Suspect G from getting back to his feet and I was able to get handcuffs on him.

After the confrontation, I asked Officer B if he was alright after being struck in the face twice. Officer B advised that he did not remember being struck in the face. During the struggle, I injured my right shoulder and it ended up being a tear in the rotator cuff. I worked my regular shifts with that injury until I had to have another orthopedic surgery a couple months later. I was off work for ten weeks to recover from that surgery.

***

I believe that I would be negligent, if I didn't include at least one funny story about prostitution and there were plenty. One common complaint from citizens that came into the department was concerning all of the prostitutes that would walk the streets in certain areas. As CPO's we would have to work prostitution operations. This fact meant that one of the CPO's would have to dress in street clothes and pick up whores. I picked up my share of whores.

There is nothing glamorous about picking up crack whores that walk the street. I used to say that I would agree to do it, but drew the line at only picking up women. There were several transvestites and a few men that also competed for the almighty dollar walking the street.

One day, my fellow officers decided that they would mess with me and called out the location of a "beautiful one in a green dress". I pretty much knew that it was going to be a man. I responded to the location and observed Suspect H, who was a black male standing on the corner wearing a green dress. I decided to break my own rule and pulled up to Suspect H at my front passenger side and put the window down. I spoke briefly to Suspect H and he climbed into the pick-up truck.

Luckily (I guess), he solicited me for sex right away and I gave the code word for uniformed officers to move in to affect an arrest. I told Suspect H that I wanted to find someplace private as I was still driving and watching my mirror for the police cruiser. I could see the cruisers coming from three blocks back and could also see Suspect H becoming nervous and feeling for the door handle in the dark. I had just started to pull away from a stop sign and was not traveling that quickly, when Suspect H sprang quickly out the front passenger window that was still open.

I grabbed onto Suspect H by his dress and kept the truck moving at ten to fifteen miles per hour. Suspect H was all of the way outside of the truck pushing off of the front passenger door with his hands and feet and screaming, "Let me go, let me go, help!" His dress had hiked up above his waist and I was not letting go of it. The cruisers were closing in from a block away and I did not let go of the dress until uniformed officer took ahold of Suspect H. I just wished that the cruiser had a dash camera, because I am quite certain that the video would have been an internet sensation.

Chapter 15

The department was still having a serious problem with officers leaving for other agencies and a large number of senior officers retiring. The authorized strength of the department was still 540 officers, but the number of sworn officers actually working at one point dropped to a staggering 430. We were missing 110 police officers on the street, or 20% of the force. Many argued that the 540 authorized number was too low in the first place. This fact meant that the remaining officers had to pick up the slack or handle all of the additional work. The patrol officers continued to take the brunt of much of the work and detectives simply had more unsolved cases pile up on their desks.

The City was questioned so often about staffing levels that they even hired an expert to complete an analysis to determine the appropriate number of sworn positions. The expert allegedly had a computer program that he could feed all of the crime date, census information, and other relevant information into and the program would provide the actual number of officers needed. The City wrote the expert a check for $150,000 and the expert told them that they needed 540 sworn police officers. What were the chances that the City administrators were exactly as intelligent as the expert's computer program? I would have told them that number for $140,000, but they never asked me.

I monitored the staffing numbers by obtaining a report from fiscal services about every six months. I would simply ask Ms. S for the spreadsheet that listed every sworn officer from the chief of police to the last new officer. Since I still had a great deal of flexibility in my CPO position, I used to work the patrol zones for officers that were refused days off for vacation. This kind of negative work environment tends to snowball and back then made many of the newly hired officers quit and go to work at neighboring agencies.

***

I was working an evening shift of a patrol officer in District Three, so he could have a vacation day. I was dispatched to a call titled "trouble with individual" to a small neighborhood convenience store. Upon arrival, I spoke to the clerk and he advised that there was a drunk black female that was causing a disturbance, and she left with a large pickle jar that belonged to the store. The clerk provided the last known direction of the female was eastbound from the store.

I circulated the neighborhood for the female suspect for a couple minutes and eventually drove through an alley to the east. I observed the female in the rear yard of an abandoned house with her arm almost elbow deep in the large pickle jar filled with juice. The suspect was fumbling to locate one of the last six pickles in the jar and was extremely intoxicated. I had the female return to the store with me along with her pickle jar. The clerk simply took the pickle jar from the suspect, placed it back on the deli counter to sell the remaining pickles, and advised that he did not want to pursue any prosecution. I instructed the female to walk home and not return to the store that evening. I always referred to this story as the great pickle caper.

***

I worked a dayshift patrol zone for another officer that was denied a vacation day. At the beginning of any dayshift, there are normally a few late reported burglaries that dayshift patrol officers are dispatched to handle. After the initial calls there is usually a brief period of quiet. The majority of the dayshift officers were senior officers and they were not looking to stir up too much trouble. It was during this quiet period that I simply went and parked my cruiser behind a neighborhood restaurant that had not opened yet.

As I was sitting there, I observed a full size white Ford van, driven by a younger black male, pull from the south and meet with a 35 year old Hispanic male that was riding a bike. The bike rider, Suspect J, rolled up to the driver window of the van handed the van driver some U.S. currency. The black male in the van handed Suspect J something small into his right hand. Suspect J cupped the object in his right hand, looked at it, and touched it with the index finger of his left hand to manipulate it. Next, Suspect J took his cupped right hand, slipped it into his right pocket, and shook it to make the small object fall. There was no question in my mind that this was the purchase of a crack cocaine rock.

At that moment, the black male looked up to see me watching them from approximately twenty yards away. I put my cruiser into gear and the black male raced away in a westbound direction. I assumed that the black male was not going to stop for my cruiser based on his initial driving, so I focused on Suspect J, who was now riding eastbound on the avenue. I called for a back-up unit and did not get a response. The dispatcher advised that she believed everyone was "tied up" and she would try to locate a unit from another district. I continued after Suspect J and initiated a traffic stop on his bicycle. I was still hoping to get a back-up unit, but had not heard anything else.

I approached Suspect J on foot and distracted him by asking about his bicycle. I advised Suspect J that there had recently been a bicycle that was stolen and I wanted to make sure that he was not riding the stolen bike. Suspect J was still straddling the bike and I knew that he would be limited in his physical maneuvering if I handcuffed him in this position. I continued to talk about the bike and the fact that it was probably not the right bicycle, but explained that I was handcuffing him briefly. Suspect J was cooperative and I placed him into handcuffs. Next, I asked Suspect J to step off of the bicycle and I started walking him toward my cruiser, where I intended to search his right front pocket in a safe position.

The dispatcher advised that she found a back-up unit from District Two and they were in route. I had ahold of Suspect J with my left hand as I reached my hand into his right front pocket and retrieved a single crack cocaine rock. I placed the evidence on the trunk of my vehicle and advised Suspect J that he was under arrest for possession of cocaine. Without warning, Suspect J pushed me backward by barreling into me with his left shoulder, reached his cuffed hands around his right side, and lunged to destroy the crack cocaine rock sitting on my trunk. I pulled Suspect J away from the cruiser and the evidence and a struggle ensued. A suspect still has the ability to fight and to hurt an officer even if he is in handcuffs.

Eventually, I was able to get Suspect J on the ground and sprayed him with "pepper spray". I advised over the radio that I needed my back-up unit to "step it up", meaning to respond in an emergency mode. Officer D arrived from District Two to assist me in putting Suspect J into the rear of my cruiser. I loaded the suspect's bike into Officer D's cruiser and transported Suspect J to the jail.

I believe that I was called to court more times on this case than any other case in my career. Initially, I had the standard State Attorney investigation, where the charges are presented to the State. Next, I received a subpoena for a "Motion to Suppress" the evidence, which I testified at and the defense lost. Then, I received a subpoena for a deposition, which is also standard in every felony offense that is going to trial. I also received a subpoena for trial, where I testified and Suspect J was found to be guilty. Next, I received a subpoena to come and testify in another county, for civil family court, where I had to testify to a civil judge in a child custody battle between Suspect J and his ex-wife.

Finally, I received a notice from the State Attorney General's office that the case had been forwarded to them for review to continue to an appeals court.

With all of that court I certainly remembered Suspect J's name. I was later advised by Officer P that Suspect J's mother actually worked at the City radio shop and I recalled seeing her at all of Suspect J's court appearances. I almost never read the newspaper or see any obituaries, but for some reason I looked at the obituaries one Sunday morning. I read the obituary of Suspect J and assumed that he had committed suicide, based on his age and all of his problems.

***

I was on patrol in the early afternoon within my CPO zone when a black Mercedes 600 series flashed the headlights and then pulled up beside me as I stopped. There was a couple in their mid-thirties sitting in the front seat that were professionally dressed and an approximate 65 year old white female sitting in the back seat. The male driver advised that they were realtors and the female in the rear seat was their client that wanted to ask me a question. I turned my attention to the female in the rear seat. The female advised that she was from out of town and her realtors were showing her a residence within the same block that we were sitting in and she provided the address and wanted to know what the neighborhood was like.

I looked at the realtors with shock and then turned my attention back to the female. I stated, "Well, let me describe it to you like this. Most of the shootings that do occur center around narcotics, so as long as you are not dealing with narcotics you should be able to avoid them. However, there are houses that occasionally do have stray rounds that hit them. There are a great number of prostitutes and transients that are in the area that tend to contribute to an increased level of other crimes." I had planned on continuing my

131

description, when the female interrupted me stating, "Officer, officer I think I have heard enough. Thank you for your time." The windows went up on the Mercedes as it drove away and I hope she fired her realtors.

***

I was working a dayshift and a call was dispatched that there was a burglary to an officer's home. The off-duty officer was a witness and they called in a description of the suspect vehicle. Initially, the dispatcher advised that it was a gold colored Hornet driven by a black male, but Officer T located a gold colored Ford Taurus speeding away from the area. Officer T pulled behind that vehicle, called out the tag, and attempted a traffic stop. The vehicle did not stop and no pursuit was authorized. The call had occurred in another District, so I monitored both radio channels.

I started researching information from the tag on the vehicle. The vehicle was registered to a black female at an address within my district. I advised the dispatcher and she sent two officers to that address in an attempt to locate the suspects. I continued researching and found the female's license gave another address in District Three within the City. I also had the dispatcher from that District send units to that address. Both of those addresses were checked and the vehicle was not located.

Next, I located a boyfriend of the registered owner of the Ford and found an address for him right outside of our City. I advised this information over the air and units were sent to that location. At that time, we did not have the ability to access photos from the cruiser computer, so I advised responding units that I would pull a photo of the potential suspect from the station. Officers located the suspect vehicle at that address just outside the City and I brought photos of the potential suspect to that scene.

Officers had made contact with a black female at that apartment, but she was talking with them through a window and denying that anyone else was inside her apartment. After about 35 minutes, the female advised that she would allow officers to search her apartment for the suspect. Officer L and I went inside the apartment and the female stated, "I told you no one is in here." We searched the apartment and as soon as I went into the bedroom, I felt the suspect's thigh with my left foot as he was hiding right under the edge of the double bed. I advised Officer L and units on the radio that there was someone hiding under the bed. I went to the opposite side of the bed and started challenging the suspect to show his hands and come out from under the bed. After a minute, the suspect came out and was arrested without incident.

I guess they thought we would never look under the bed. The female was also arrested later. She became combative and hit and kicked officers.

***

I was working another off-duty assignment at the bar that no one else wanted to work. Earlier in my shift on the street, I became aware of Officer H issuing probable cause for Suspect F, who fled from her traffic stop in a 1983 white Oldsmobile Cutlass Supreme. The suspect lived within my CPO zone, so Officer H had given the information to me.

There was a large crowd of approximately 200 people at the bar with vehicles filling the parking lots and the surrounding streets. I observed the suspect vehicle parked in the east parking lot of the bar and I informed Officer D, who was working the bar with me. We continued watching for the suspect or anyone else leaving in the vehicle. At 0145 hours the lights of the bar were turned on bright and everyone started to leave. I called for a couple more units to assist us in case we located the suspect. Almost everyone had left the bar and the surrounding streets and the white Oldsmobile was sitting by itself. A few minutes later, Suspect F walked out of the bar with the bouncer and started walking to his vehicle.

I waited for Suspect F to open his driver door before approaching him, so I could trap him in within the door opening. Suspect F immediately started screaming obscenities about how we can't stop him and started making threats. Almost immediately Suspect F reached into his front right pants pocket with his right hand. I trapped his right hand in the pocket, while still attempting to maintain control of him. Officer D was right there with me and if you were in a physical confrontation, Officer D was one of the officers that you wanted by your side. We continued to struggle at maintaining control of Suspect F and I continued to keep his right hand trapped in his pocket. I heard Officer S state over the radio that we were struggling with the suspect on the east side of the bar and knew that additional units would respond to help.

I never let go of Suspect F as he attempted to spin, hit, kick, and pull away from us, and I never released my hold on his right hand still trapped in the pocket. Eventually, we took Suspect F to the ground, cuffed the left arm, and slowly pulled his right hand out of his pocket for handcuffing. Upon a search incident to arrest, I located a two shot, .22 caliber, derringer in the Suspect F's front right pocket and a tube with 53 crack cocaine rocks in his front left pocket. I always thought about that arrest as one of those shots was for me and one was for Officer D, but God was with us that day.

***

I was riding with Officer B, another CPO, one evening. The dispatcher provided information about a call from another district that was a carjacking. The dispatcher advised that a known subject, Suspect W, took an elderly female's vehicle and threatened her.

Upon hearing the name of Suspect W, a patrol Officer B came on the radio and provided additional information about the suspect. The patrol officer advised that he was in traffic court on the prior evening and he remembered the suspect because he looked like Rush Limbaugh, the radio host. The Patrol Officer B advised further the approximate location that Suspect W lived and that he was 6 foot tall and weighed 275 pounds.

We were not too far away from the area where Suspect W was believed to live, so I advised Officer B to drive up to that area. We had just started down the avenue eastbound, when I observed "Rush Limbaugh" walking westbound on the south sidewalk. I yelled to Officer B to stop our cruiser and jumped out with the suspect. I asked, "What is your name?" and the suspect replied with the name of Suspect W. We placed the suspect into handcuffs less than 30 minutes after he violently took an elderly female victim's vehicle. The vehicle was located a half a block to the east of our location and was returned to the elderly victim. Suspect W ended up pleading guilty to a battery on the elderly charge and received two years house arrest, followed by two years of probation. Rush Limbaugh was given credit for the arrest by the judge on the case, as well as from the local newspaper.

Chapter 16

Even early in my career, I believe I was recognized as an officer that was competent to do the right thing and I had a better understanding of how things in the criminal justice system worked, and how things worked within our department, than many other new officers. Sergeants were supposed to read and sign off on certain types of reports, especially arrest reports. No matter which sergeant I took my reports to for a signature, they simply blindly signed them and I would observe them read other officer's reports before providing a signature. About this time in my career, I had about five years with the department and even senior officers would actually come to me with questions.

***

I was working an off-duty assignment at a baseball game. We worked the traffic coming into the game and then traffic as everyone exited and usually had a long break in the middle. The break time was normally used for a workout and pick up some lunch.

I received a call from Sergeant M asking if I was working. I explained to him that I was working the baseball game and he asked if I would do him a favor during the break. Sergeant M asked me to respond to a church and speak with an individual who was a former officer. Sure, sounded easy enough. Upon arrival at the church, I found the former officer, Mr. H, and spoke with him. Mr. H advised that he was now an elder at the church and a group of the elders suspected that the current preacher was stealing money from the church and they wanted to trespass him off of the church property. The preacher was inside the church itself holding Wednesday night service. This was not a simple favor.

I obtained a great deal of information from the elders of the church. I initially asked how the church was formed. After learning it was a corporation, I requested the Articles of Incorporation, the By-laws, and minutes from any board of directors (or elder's) meetings. I had to quickly read through all of these documents to determine who is actually supposed to have control of the church and its' assets. The elders also informed me that the new pastor was the grandson of the original founder of the church, but the original founder was deceased. The elders advised that the new pastor had spent $315,000 of the church's savings over the course of a single year.

I was able to determine that the elders actually did have the authority to remove the pastor from the property and they wanted me to trespass him, so he would not return. I entered the church, interrupting the service, and called the pastor outside. I did complete the trespassing and watched as the pastor drove off in a $65,000 Mercedes, owned by the church. The following day, someone told me that I made the newspaper, and I read that there were injunctions being filed in civil court. I had to advise Sergeant M, "No more simple favors."

***

I was working an evening shift as a CPO, when a call was dispatched as a domestic battery victim standing on the street corner. I was not too far away, so I told the dispatcher that I would take care of the call. Upon arrival, I observed the white female victim and started to take down her statements.

I quickly learned that the offense occurred in another jurisdiction and the female was simply left here by the suspect, boyfriend. I advised the dispatcher that I would transport the female victim to the other jurisdiction. While in route, the victim continued to explain her story to me. The victim advised that she had been dating the suspect for a couple of years and that they were now living together in the neighboring jurisdiction. The victim advised that the suspect was

Muslim, born in Iraq, and he did not have the same respect of women that you would find here in America. I met with a female officer in the neighboring city and she completed the investigation. Eventually, I observed all of the victim's injuries, which included solid bruising from the center of the victim's back, across the buttocks, and slightly onto the victim's thighs. The victim advised that the suspect frequently beat her with a leather belt.

The other officer issued probable cause for battery and I learned that the suspect worked in a band that played at a bar within our City every weekend. I could not believe the injury and abuse that the victim had sustained and I was going to make a point to ensure that the suspect was arrested. I responded to the bar and left my information for the manager to contact myself or the police department's communications center when the suspect showed up to play.

Then, I received what I always referred to as the "morning after call". This call was commonly made to police officers the next day following a domestic dispute or battery. The victims would always call with an attempt to change their story, or minimize what the suspect did, or to tell the officer that they no longer wanted to prosecute. Due to the extensive bruising, I did not expect the call as usual, but the call was made by the victim. I listened to the voicemail and heard the victim say, "I decided that he really is sorry and that he really did not hit me that hard and I think that we are going to stay together." I never received a call from the bar and never heard from the female again.

**

Normally, someone that is on house arrest does not call the police as a victim, because they are always at home. I heard a call dispatched of a theft of a house arrest monitoring unit and responded to take the call. Upon arrival, I spoke with the victim and obtained her statement. The victim advised that she had purchased a 150 foot phone cord, so she could take her house arrest monitoring unit all the way out to the street corner. The victim advised that she was outside with the unit and she went back inside her residence to use the restroom. The victim claimed that when she came back outside, that the unit was missing.

I contacted her probation officer and he advised that they did receive notice that the unit had been disconnected from the phone line. The officer advised that the unit had a GPS on it and he showed it to be approximately one block away. I walked in the direction of the GPS signal and the officer advised that he could set off an audible alarm when I was close. I arrived to a corner house with a half address and the officer set off the alarm. I could hear the unit going off inside the half address, so I went and knocked on the door. I spoke with Suspect O, who advised that he did not know what I was talking about and then admitted that the unit was inside his house. Eventually, Suspect O admitted that he took the unit, but had no idea what the unit was used for.

I arrested Suspect O, returned the unit to the victim, and transported Suspect O to jail. Since the probation officer advised that the unit was worth $2,500, the suspect was charged with grand theft. I attended the State Attorney investigation and the State informed me that they probably would not file any charges.

***

Within my CPO zone there were many individuals that I had arrested more than once and certainly many individuals that I would have dealings with on more than one occasion. One of those subjects was Suspect K. Suspect K was always listed as the suspect in numerous offenses, but most of them never proceeded to court due the victims not being credible. It is hard to prosecute a case when your star witness is a crack

140

addict that always lies to the police. I remember numerous reports of listing Suspect K as the suspect in batteries, car thefts, and I even had a fleeing and eluding offense with Suspect K.

On one occasion Detective G and Detective N asked me to go to Suspect K's house to assist with his arrest. The detectives went to the front door and they asked me to remain in the alley in case he ran on foot. Sure enough one minute after they spoke to him at the front door, Suspect K fled from the back door. At one point in the foot chase, I observed Suspect K run up a slight incline in a yard and jump over a four foot chain link fence with no effort and without touching the fence. Luckily for me, there was an open gate about ten feet to the left. I chased him for two blocks calling it out on the radio and other uniformed officers were able to catch him.

Eventually months later, several serious charges were finally filed by the State Attorney's Office and Suspect K had active warrants. Suspect K must have pissed off the wrong person in the neighborhood, because a call was made to the police where we could find Suspect K. Suspect K was located by other officers in an alley. Suspect K had been beat up and was wrapped up and secured by a roll of duct tape. I wish I could have seen that scene. Suspect K was never released from jail and later plead out to 25 years in prison.

***

One evening shift, I worked a narcotics operation with both my department's narcotics unit and the county's narcotic unit. One of the Sheriff's younger deputies had made a narcotic purchase and he was trying to identify a black female prostitute that he had purchased narcotics from. Someone had taken their eyes off of the female and she was probably picked up by a "John" for prostitution and disappeared.

I heard the description given by the deputy, which included the fact that she was wearing a bikini top. I met with the deputy, because I knew a 21 year old black female prostitute that always worked while wearing a bikini top in that area. I pulled out my large binder of usual suspects and flipped to the page of a known black female with a street name of "Peaches". Upon seeing my photo, the deputy became very animated and exclaimed, "Oh, my God that is her, that is so her!" Next, I simply stated that I wasn't sure it would be her because the suspect in the picture was only 21 years old. The deputy quickly changed his decision and stated, "Well if she is 21 then that is not my suspect."

I could not believe the deputy's attitude toward identifying suspects. An officer should be absolutely certain in his identifications of suspects and when you are not able to make a 100% call, well that is the way it goes. With every arrest you are taking away someone's freedom, so you have to be certain, especially if you are making that call yourself.

***

One day when I was patrolling within my CPO zone, I observed an occupied vehicle parked near an intersection, and I knew I had not seen it before. I ran the tag on the vehicle as I passed by and observed a black male leaned back in the driver's seat. The intersection was where three different roads came together. I drove out of sight and then drove through the intersection on a different road. When I was almost out of sight again, the brake lights came on and the vehicle drove off southbound. I had taken a good look at the driver when I drove past the second time, because I approached from the front, shining my headlight into the vehicle.

I watched as the vehicle continued to leave the area. Eventually, I caught up to the vehicle and I am certain he knew I was approaching, because he drove right

142

through a stop sign. I initiated a traffic stop on the vehicle and called for a back-up unit to assist me. The vehicle began to accelerate away from me and I knew that he planned to flee. I was in the middle of a block, where there was nowhere for me to turn away from being behind the vehicle, as our department rules required, so I simply stopped in the middle of the roadway. I watched as the suspect vehicle approached the next intersection, where he had a stop sign. The suspect planned on simply running through that stop sign, but he did not realize that the street created a huge rise in the road. The suspect hit the rise of the intersection and the vehicle jumped in the air and landed clear on the opposite side of that street out of control. The suspect kept overcorrecting in both directions and eventually glanced off the side of a telephone pole.

I was still sitting in the center of the block watching from a distance of about one and a half blocks away. I realized that the vehicle stopped moving, so I drove up to it and called for another unit. The lights of the vehicle were still on as I approached on foot. When I checked the vehicle, there was no one inside. I called for a K-9 unit to attempt to track for the suspect with negative results. A search of the vehicle revealed two large paper grocery bags full of marijuana, a small amount of crack cocaine, and a semi-automatic handgun.

I investigated the tag for prior stops and offenses and eventually I identified the suspect that I had observed. I issued probable cause for his arrest and arrested him at a later date. The vehicle was a Ford and they had a safety shut off to the fuel pump, when the vehicles received an impact. The crash into the telephone pole shut off the fuel pump, so the suspect could no longer operate the vehicle until he pushed the fuel pump reset switch in the rear compartment. Thanks for stopping my suspect Ford! Sergeant Q was so impressed with my actions and follow-up that he submitted my actions for a national law enforcement award. Luckily, I did not win; I am not the award type.

***

I had a small neighborhood convenience store that was inside my zone on a fairly busy street. One evening it was robbed by a black male with an AR-15 rifle. Approximately one week later, the clerk observed the same black male come into the store, so he picked up a .38 caliber revolver that was kept at the store. The black male stepped up to the register and this time pulled out a semi-automatic handgun to rob the store a second time. The clerk shot the suspect right through the eye socket and then called "911".

The suspect was still alive when officers and rescue units arrived, but died later at the hospital. Officer O was one of the responding units and was an excellent police officer with a morbid sense of humor. Officer O leaned over the suspect, as the suspect laid on the floor moaning in agony, and asked, "Did you see it coming?"

Later that week, I had to attend a monthly neighborhood meeting, where I presented the crime statistics to residents. The meetings were attended by elderly black females that had lived in the neighborhood all of their lives and were somewhat trapped amongst all the crime. One of the residents made a comment to me that I will never forget. The female stated, "That clerk did not have to shoot the man, he was only robbing him."

***

I was asked if I would allow patrol Officer S to ride with me for one shift to observe what I did as a CPO. During that shift, I observed a subject that was not known to me standing at a known drug house. I made a point to get to know any citizens that I observed within my CPO zone. I observed that subject leave from that

144

residence on a bicycle and commit a traffic infraction. The bicycle was also not registered with the City, which was an ordinance violation. I initiated a traffic stop on the bicycle, but the black male was not stopping for the traffic stop. I continued following the path of the black male as he rode along the sidewalk as fast as he could.

I continued to advise the dispatcher that I needed back-up officers to respond and was advised again that there were none available. The black male rode toward a busy two lane avenue and turned eastbound. I continued following him to a point where I observed a wide entrance to a city recreation center. I pulled ahead of the bicycle, into the entrance, and cut off the bicycles path. I jumped from my cruiser and grabbed ahold of the black male, who was 5 foot nine and weighed 250 pounds.

The black male was pushing and attempting to break free from me as I struggled to take him to the ground. Initially, we were fighting on the sidewalk and then the struggle spilled into the avenue. I was finally able to take him to the ground literally on top of the double yellow line of the avenue, which stopped all traffic. Officer S was also in the struggle, but was not able to get either hand behind the suspect's back. I notified the dispatcher of our fighting and finally units were responding. I sprayed the suspect with "pepper spray" twice before finally getting him into handcuffs. The back-up units arrived to assist me in getting the suspect into my cruiser.

The arrest scene was approximately 50 yards from the Uhuru national headquarters, which was a group that basically did not like the police even being in their neighborhood. The stopped traffic and police sirens made a group of ten individuals, including the Uhuru leader, Mr. W. come from the headquarters, to see what was happening. One of my back-up officers that responded was a black male named Officer S. Officer S asked the group of ten if they would not stand so close to the cruiser with the suspect and they all responded with comments of "fuck you" and "We can stand on the sidewalk if we want."

About 30 seconds later, the suspect in my cruiser kicked out the rear driver's side door window, showering the group with tiny cubes of glass. The group started to back away and Officer S eloquently asked, "My goodness, are you all alright that looks like a lot of glass?" This only prompted more cursing from the group.

Chapter 17

At the end of my sixth year, I decided to submit an application for an opening in the department's Special Investigations Unit, or SIU. The SIU detectives all worked in an undercover surveillance capacity and worked active crime patterns and located wanted suspects. SIU was an elite undercover detective unit, the best of the best. The unit not only had a stellar reputation within our department, but the surrounding agencies and counties in Florida knew of the work that the unit was able to accomplish. SIU detectives were always working the most pressing case or the most wanted individual of the day. Each and every day brought new challenges.

The unit obviously wasn't simply available to any officer that wanted to join. SIU consisted of a Sergeant and seven detectives that worked as a team to combat the crime patterns or locate wanted suspects. Everyone in the unit worked in an undercover capacity and drove undercover vehicles. Ironically, my memorandum was initially denied, similar to when I applied to my CPO position. A couple months later, I received a call at home from Sergeant Q on a Thursday and he asked, "Hey Mike, are you still interested in going to SIU." I replied, "Absolutely" and Sergeant Q stated, "Congratulations, you will officially start working as a detective in SIU on Monday." Once again, my work ethic and reputation helped me to avoid a silly interview.

Now, I already knew Sergeant M in SIU and all of the detectives, because I worked with them as much as I could in my position as a CPO. I knew how well the unit worked together on the street and the great accomplishments that they were able to achieve. What I didn't realize from the outside, was the fact that you needed to prove your worth every day in the unit, because the unit was full of Alpha dogs. Since the unit was only comprised of a total of eight people, there wasn't any room for someone that would not pull their weight.

The first challenge was learning all of the new surveillance techniques that I had never been exposed to actually using. I was told right from the beginning by Sergeant M that I would not feel comfortable with surveillance until I had worked in the unit for an entire year. There ended up being a lot of truth to that statement. I felt like a brand new officer trying to learn everything again. Simply working in an undercover capacity on the street creates a list of new challenges. Undercover detectives do not wear an officer's duty belt, so I had to learn new ways to access all of my equipment. Even using the police radio was different in the unit.

***

A great deal of my first two months was spent doing training. We also made several arrests, recovered stolen vehicles, and located a few wanted subjects. I believe the first big or active crime pattern that we worked was a sexual battery to an elderly victim. We obtained all the information from the Sex Crimes Unit.

The victim was an 85 year old white female, who lived alone in a small 600 square foot single story home not too far from downtown. The victim initially reported a burglary to her residence in October, where a black male had entered the home one evening, wrapped a towel around the victim's face, and force her to fondle his penis. The suspect left after taking some money. Two months later, the victim reported another offense in the evening, where the black male entered her residence, wrapped a sheet around her head, and forced intercourse to her. The suspect left again after taking more money from the victim. A few days later, the victim reported a third burglary to her residence that occurred when she was not home. The unknown suspect took many of the victim's Christmas gifts.

We obtained the information and started working the case four days after Christmas. The victim was relocated to another residence, but everything in the victim's residence was kept the same including the lighting. We set up surveillance covering the front and rear of the victim's residence with primary spots and had the remainder of the detectives around the perimeter. The residence was a couple blocks away from a main thoroughfare in the City, so the surrounding area was a little active all night. There was a little reluctance to working the case from a couple senior detectives, because it didn't seem highly probable that the suspect would return.

On about the fourth night, I moved to take the primary position on the front of the residence. I met with Detective N, who was the most senior in the unit, and I was taking the position from him. Detective N stayed with me for a couple minutes and we talked. I remember Detective N telling me, "Just think, Biz, at any minute the suspect could walk up to the residence to break inside and we will all move in and take him into custody." That type of positive attitude can be very contagious.

On the ninth night, everyone in the unit was losing confidence that the suspect would return. On this night, I was covering the primary position at the rear of the residence and it was about 0330 hours. I had been staring at this residence for nine nights in a row and was honestly half asleep. All of the sudden, I observed the black male suspect looking into the north window on the east side of the residence. I thought I was imagining things at first, but then I watched as the suspect moved quickly to the southern window on that same east side. I notified units over the radio of what I was watching. The suspect was only up to the residence for about 45 seconds and then walked east toward the alley out of sight.

I moved from the primary position at the rear to move in to affect the arrest of the black male. Next, I observed the suspect walking quickly northbound in the alley behind the residence. The alley continued north and ended in a parking lot of an assisted living facility. I followed behind the suspect calling out his movements as we continued toward the rear of that facility. The suspect disappeared into a dark corner of the building and started to come out of it with his bicycle that he had stored there. I identified myself as a police officer as I took ahold of the suspect's left arm. The suspect began to resist my efforts and commands and tried to pull away to ride off on his bicycle. I threw the suspect to the ground and punched the suspect several times in the right rear of his rib cage. This force took all of the fight out of the suspect and Detective C helped me handcuff him.

Sergeant M notified the Sex Crime Detectives that we had made an arrest for Loitering and Prowling. Detective M responded to the station to interview the suspect and establish her case for the burglaries and the sexual offenses. The fingerprint technician, Ms. D, was also called in from home to run a comparison from a partial print lifted after one of the offenses. The suspect denied any involvement in any of the previous offenses, but the partial print was a match to the suspect. The suspect was charged with all of the offenses.

Months later, they were also able to establish a DNA link to other evidence recovered in the previous offenses. The suspect pled to all of the charges and received a sentence of life in prison.

I believe that this case established the foundation for my desire to work active or in-progress crimes. I had responded to plenty of in-progress crimes after being dispatched as a uniformed officer, but being there from the start for the entire offense was different. Prior to this case, my favorite thing to do was to track down and locate wanted subjects that did not want to be found. I never lost that desire either, but catching suspects while they are in the process of trying to victimize others is very addicting.

***

About six months after I came to the unit, the chief approved one additional detective for the unit, so Detective J was assigned to SIU. This transfer meant that there were eight detectives and now each detective would have a partner. Usually, we rode with our partner on the street, but some cases demanded that we were assigned by ourselves. The best thing about the unit was that we always worked together as a team.

Detective J was the first detective in our unit to use a Taser on a suspect after they were issued to officers on the department. We had located a stolen vehicle and were conducting a surveillance of the vehicle. The suspects had pulled into the rear parking lot of a duplex off of the alley. The suspects walked off on foot eastbound to a small convenience store before we could identify the driver. Detective J and I were assigned on foot at the parking lot of the duplex to make the call when the suspects returned to the vehicle.

We were set up and waiting for the suspects to return to the vehicle along the east side of the duplex, because that was the path the suspects took when they left. The suspects surprised Detective J by walking up behind him from the west side of the duplex. Detective J simply asked the suspects if he could have a ride. I notified the other detectives that the suspects had returned. As the suspects were getting into the stolen vehicle, Detective J challenged the driver suspect. The suspect turned to run and Detective J hit him with the Taser. The suspect went down and became compliant

151

right away. The alley was dark and quiet and the light and sound from the Taser put on quite a show. The other suspect ran north on foot and was caught by other detectives in the unit. The Taser eventually became a very effective tool for all officers, because it decreased the number of officers involved in physical confrontations and therefore decreased officer injuries. Even the threat of the Taser would cause many suspects to comply with an officer's commands.

***

I personally only hit two suspects with the Taser, but one of them could possibly have been the best hit with a Taser of anyone on the police department.

We were conducting surveillance on a stolen Ford Mustang. The vehicle was occupied by two black male juveniles and had been driving all over the City. The vehicle pulled up to the front of a convenience store and the driver went inside. Detective C and I went into the convenience store seconds behind the driver, as other detectives boxed the vehicle in the parking lot. Since we were dressed in undercover clothing and always carrying a gun, I always made a point to quickly show my badge to the convenient store clerk prior to taking action inside the store. I always assumed that every clerk had a handgun under the counter.

We handcuffed the driver inside and I walked him out to the front sidewalk. Once outside, I could see that the front seat passenger had jumped into the driver's seat of the Mustang and was attempting to drive it away. Sergeant M had his undercover vehicle behind the suspect vehicle boxing it in, but the suspect tried to push backward and then pulled forward. When the suspect pulled forward the Mustang pushed up against a metal pole filled with concrete that was protecting the glass front of the store.

I pulled the handcuffed, arrested suspect over toward the Mustang and held onto him with my left hand. I took my Taser out with my right hand and hit the other suspect with the Taser as he sat in the driver's seat. The suspect's entire body immediately went erect and his foot pushed against the accelerator. The vehicle was braced against the strong metal pole and the rear tires started to do an incredible burnout. The front of Sergeant M's vehicle ended up covered with debris and tar from burning tires. The Taser is set for five seconds and that is a pretty long burnout. The parking lot was filled with smoke and visibility dropped to about two feet in front of your face. The incident caused several groups of loitering individuals to leave the area quickly.

As soon as the Taser shut off, Detective S took the arrested suspect that I was holding with my left hand and I reached inside the Mustang and shut the car off. At that exact moment, another detective shattered the front passenger window to gain access to the inside of the Mustang from the passenger side and particles of glass flew and hit my left eye. The two suspects were transported to jail and I went to the emergency room with actual cuts on my eyeball.

***

I was riding with Detective N during Christmas season one year. Both of us had a strong appreciation of Christmas music, so we always had it playing as we circulated the City looking for crime. Every now and then when a favorite song would play, Detective N would "inadvertently" key up the police radio so everyone on the channel could enjoy the music.

We located a stolen vehicle that had several suspects inside and we were in a very active surveillance. As we raced through the busy City streets, the Christmas music was still playing in the background from our truck's radio. I remember the song "It's the Most Wonderful Time of the Year" coming on the radio being sung by Andy Williams. Detective N had just driven over a curb and was cutting through the parking lot of a

153

Citgo gas station to avoid some traffic that was backed up from a traffic light. I stated, "Hey you know Detective N, this could be the scene from a movie where there are flashing back and forth from the "car chase" that we were involved in and to the interior of our truck listening to Andy Williams." We laughed so hard it was difficult to stay in the surveillance.

***

We monitored all of the crime throughout the entire City to ensure that we would pick up on any crime patterns early. If we were not working a specific pattern, then we would simply drive around and look for crime. One of the detectives coined the acronym D.A.D.N. or "Dad'n", driving around doing nothing. Of course, this was only a joke, because there was always something to work and one of our detectives was usually in the right place at the right time for all of us all to, eventually, get involved.

We also monitored the three patrol radio channels, so we could respond to anything that was in-progress. Unfortunately, we normally only had five cars working the street and sometimes we wouldn't be close enough. I remember specifically, one shooting call that was dispatched that we were all disappointed that we were not close. A suspect entered a Radio Shack looked around and then just starting shooting people.

The suspect was a 25 year old white male and he entered the store with a .40 caliber handgun. The suspect shot two clerks and a 19 year old white female customer. Another customer was able to escape from the store and call the police. The call was dispatched as an active shooter, but none of our detectives were close enough to help. The victims were in the wrong place at the wrong time and we were in the wrong place to be of any assistance.

Uniformed officers responded to the scene to find that the suspect had turned his gun on himself and committed suicide. The 19 year old female and a 23 year old male clerk died in surgery.

***

There were an extremely high number of auto thefts in the City. The City had approximately 250,000 residents and at one point had about 200 vehicles stolen in an average month. The majority of the thefts were teenagers taking joy rides and then dumping the vehicles when they ran out of gas. My facetious solution was to inform all city residents to never drive around with more than an eighth of a tank of gas. I was also quick to point out that we already had the suspects contained within the boundaries of the City.

The sergeant in auto theft at the time was receiving a great deal of pressure from the staff and City leaders, but no one was willing to allow officers to combat the problems more aggressively. The rules and regulations at the time prevented any officer from pursuing any stolen vehicle that did not want to stop for cruisers, and police officers could not box-in any of the stolen vehicles. The rules actually stated that police officers were required to leave an "avenue of escape" for vehicles on a stop, and escape they would.

Representatives from several automobile insurance companies met with the police department's staff and with Sergeant C. The companies offered to equip a "bait car" to combat the auto theft problem. Other, larger cities had great luck in arresting suspects after they would steal the bait car. The car that was donated took about three months for the maintenance shop to equip with the camera, GPS, and monitoring equipment. Our unit was tasked with being responsible for operating the vehicle and parking it at strategic locations.

Unfortunately, the one bait car was not any more desirable than any of the other 500,000 vehicles in the City. Also, the staff of the police department were so concerned about the liability of auto theft suspects driving in a vehicle that the department legally parked on a City street, that they would not allow the vehicle to simply be left in public without our team of detectives watching it.

Prior to working with the bait car, we were easily arresting ten to fifteen auto theft suspects a month. The bait car ended up being a complete bust and not a single arrest was made from all that effort. When we worked with the bait car, our team of detectives were pulled away from our normal routine and making other arrests. We worked less and less with the bait car and eventually the department returned the car to the insurance companies. Our unit was finally granted the ability to box-in stolen vehicles and violent felons. The vehicle boxing maneuver resulted in countless arrests.

Chapter 18

We identified a commercial burglary pattern, where a suspect was breaking into convenience stores and taking Newport cigarettes. Senior detectives in the unit remembered arresting a black male suspect a few years earlier with the same M.O. (modus operandi). We met with burglary detectives who had copies of video surveillance from the burglaries and it appeared to be the same individual, Suspect W.

We started working surveillance of Suspect W and on the first night he went out "shopping". Suspect W left his known residence on a bicycle and started riding. It was after midnight, and it is true nothing good happens after midnight. Suspect W rode his bicycle for about three miles and went straight to a small neighborhood convenience store. Some suspects are careful to check the surrounding area for any witnesses, but not Suspect W.

Suspect W rode onto the parking lot and went right up to the front glass of the business. Suspect W pulled a three foot metal pole from a bag that he brought with him and started banging it against the front door glass. Detective C had taken a position in the neighboring parking lot behind a fence and was calling out Suspect W's actions. Each time Detective C would key his radio up to say he is banging on the door, we could hear the bang come across the radio. Suspect W pounded on the door with the pole about five times before he realized he was not going to make it past the safety glass.

Suspect W jumped onto his bicycle and started racing out of the area in the same direction which he came to the store. We continued surveillance on Suspect W and had called for uniformed officers to respond to make an arrest. K-9 Officer T arrived in the area and started to drive northbound on the street where Suspect W was riding. Detective C was already in the middle of the block and ran up to Suspect W who was still on the bicycle. Somehow, either Detectives C's takedown or Suspect W's resistance threw both of them in front of the oncoming K-9 cruiser. The K-9 cruiser drove right over the top of Suspect W on the bicycle and also either struck Detective C knocking him away or partially drove on top of Detective C.

We all moved in as K-9 Officer T notified us as to what happened and rescue was called to the scene of an "officer down". Detective C was initially knocked out cold, but became partially responsive and moaning in pain. Suspect W was tangled within the bicycle partially and I assisted separating the bicycle and handcuffing Suspect W. Suspect W initially was trying to get up off the ground, but could not speak and was having trouble breathing. I could see that Suspect W's right shin bone was bent at 90 degrees and was protruding through the skin on his leg by about four inches. I stated, "You better just concentrate on your breathing, because I don't think you are going to make it."

After rescue units treated Detective C on scene and he was transported, I responded to Detective C's residence to notify his wife. I knocked on the door and rang the doorbell, but did not receive any response. Next, I called Mrs. C on the phone and I believe she figured out the two different attempts were related. Mrs. C came to the door and I advised her of what had happened and the status of Detective C.

Suspect W proved me wrong, as he was on probation and committing other felonies in no time. About six months later, Suspect W was wanted for fleeing and eluding and we located him at a "crack motel" and placed him under arrest. Detective C was not as fortunate for it took Detective C three full years and three separate shoulder surgeries to recover enough to come back to work.

***

We were provided information from the robbery unit about Suspect E, who had a warrant for a recent bank robbery. Suspect E was already out on bond for a different felony offense and had already violated that bond by not showing up for a court appearance. Suspect E had utilized a bail bondsman to post bond and the bondsman had already been looking to arrest him.

When defendants utilize a bail bondsman they sign a contract with the bondsman. The bondsman will post the full bond for the defendant to get out of jail and the defendant pays a bond premium, usually 10% of the bond, to the bondsman and also agrees to appear for all future court dates. There also is a list of conditions that the defendant must comply with, so the bondsman can be comfortable that a defendant will show up for future court dates. If the defendant violates one of the conditions or fails to show up for a required court appearance then the bondsman can take him into custody and return him to jail. The contractual agreement also grants the right to a bail bondsman to kick down the door of the defendant's residence to arrest the defendant.

We tracked the suspect down to a nice apartment complex, but had never observed Suspect E on the property. The bondsman had been notified of the information and had responded to the scene. The bondsman decided he was going to go inside and arrest Suspect E with one of his partners. The apartment was on the second level and had a door on the ground level that opened to a long stairwell that went up to the second floor. Our unit was going to remain outside the building on a perimeter in case Suspect E decided to flee.

About one minute after the bondsman entered the door to climb the stairwell, a single gunshot was heard. The gunfire itself created an exigent circumstance that police officers could enter the apartment without a warrant, so we started to move toward the apartment entrance. As I approached the entry door, one of the bondsmen opened it and yelled that Suspect E had shot himself. One of our detectives called for rescue units to respond and I entered the stairwell with the bondsman.

I climbed the stairwell and entered the apartment to find the other bondsman speaking with Suspect E. I observed a .22 caliber handgun lying on the floor next to Suspect E and it was secured. Suspect E was moaning in pain, but was speaking clearly with us. The fact that Suspect E was even alive was shocking, because he had placed the .22 caliber handgun onto his temple and pulled the trigger. The single round went into Suspect E's head.

Detectives were called in to the scene to investigate the shooting, although it was pretty clear what had happened. Even Suspect E admitted to shooting himself and wished that the gun had a second round in it. Suspect E was taken to the hospital and it was determined the round blew out the optic nerve of both of his eyes and he would be blind forever, but would recover fine otherwise. Suspect E was later convicted and sentenced to prison for the previous bank robbery offense.

***

We worked another active bank robbery suspect that detectives were still trying to develop probable cause for the offense. There was enough evidence to put a GPS tracker on the suspect's vehicle. The problem was that he had two vehicles, so we ended up using two different GPS units. Unfortunately, the units were pretty old technology and the suspect ended up locating them on his vehicles. The signals from the units disappeared and I am sure that they were placed at the bottom of a deep body of water. The administration of the police

160

department was not very happy, because the units had cost about $8,000 each.

Once the suspect had located the GPS units, he was impossible to follow because he was always looking for someone behind him. Eventually, the robbery detectives were able to generate probable cause for his arrest and they served a search warrant at his residence. We responded to his place of employment to arrest him. We entered a large warehouse through the rear door and other detectives had entered through the front of the business. I observed the suspect walking down one of the isles of the warehouse. I called out the fictitious name of Scott to the suspect, and started walking toward him as other detectives were moving in to affect the arrest. I continued distracting him by insisting that he was Scott and that I needed his help. The suspect was taken into custody without incident.

***

One evening shift, we were notified by the U.S. Marshal Services that they had located a homicide suspect that was wanted for a homicide in the State of Georgia. Every so often we would also have other police officers from our agency that wanted to come and ride with our unit to see everything that we did. Usually, the officers would ride with me and on this shift I had Officer P riding with me.

We obtained all of the information from the Marshal Services in a briefing held on a street corner and we all responded to the apartment complex where the suspect was staying. After about an hour, the suspect came down from his apartment, climbed into his vehicle, and left. We conducted surveillance on the vehicle up to a local 7-11 gas station and the suspect pulled right in front of the entry doors.

A decision was made to box the suspect vehicle in as soon as he parked. I was set up to take the passenger side of the suspect vehicle. Everything on the vehicle box went smoothly and we were challenging the suspect and still taking him into custody. There are about eight law enforcement officers standing in the parking lot with guns drawn and a couple officers yelling commands toward the driver. An unrelated white male walks out of the 7-11 and starts to walk straight through the area where the box is occurring and into the line of fire. Detective J yells to the subject to move and walk around the activity. The white male subject is about six foot four inches tall and weighed about 350 pounds and acted like no one can tell him what to do. He says, "Fuck you" to Detective J and walks right into Detective J pushing him backward.

Now, Detective J was six foot two and weighed about 340 pounds and was not going to be battered by the subject. Detective J holstered his firearm, picked up the 350 pound white male subject, and slammed him to the pavement in the parking lot. I had to keep my attention on the homicide suspect that we were taking into custody. I approached and started handcuffing the homicide suspect. I turned around and observed both Detective J and one of the U.S. Marshal agents fighting with the white male subject to get him into handcuffs. The white male subject committed a third degree felony, to try to prove that no one could tell him what to do.

***

Since we reviewed all of the call activity in the City and all of the offense reports that were taken by police officers, sometimes we would help with various investigations. There were many times that one of our detectives would be able to contact another detective within our department to provide pertinent information or provide a specific suspect name.

One day I reviewed a robbery report from a CVS that documented a description of a white male suspect, who was driving a white Chrysler K-car. Since there weren't too many Chrysler K-cars still on the road in our City, I conducted further research on the robbery. I located one in particular that was registered to a white female, who had recently traded the vehicle for crack cocaine. I found her in another report listed with a white male named Suspect L. I looked at pictures of Suspect L and he was the robber from the CVS. I made a quick call to robbery and they developed probable cause for his arrest.

In another robbery there was a blurry picture of a gold Nissan pick-up truck, which included a partial tag and a yellow bumper sticker. I worked for a couple hours and generated a strong possible that was registered right outside our City. I was not able to check on the vehicle that I found to confirm that it had the bumper sticker, because we were tied up on anther crime pattern. I contacted one of the sergeants in patrol and had him drive to that residence out of the City and he was able to confirm it was the robbery vehicle. I made a call to robbery detectives, who interviewed the registered owner and they learned the name of the robbery suspect that the truck had been loaned to. They were able to develop probable cause for the suspect's arrest based on that information.

On another case, there was a pattern of Dunkin Donut robberies and we had a picture of a vehicle with a partial tag. Most surveillance cameras do not give the best quality images, so it was hard to tell exactly what vehicle and year the suspect vehicle was. There was also a white bumper sticker on that vehicle in a specific location that could be seen on the surveillance video. A list of about thirty matching vehicles was generated from all registered in our county. I researched for a couple hours and generated a vehicle registered out of another county, but found a local address for the registered owner and a recent report that involved the registered owner and crack cocaine. Where there was crack cocaine there was always additional crime.

We all went and checked for the bumper sticker on the list of potential vehicles. I had already advised everyone that I was 99% certain that the vehicle that I located from the other county was the right one and had also developed the name of a related black male that fit the description of the robbery suspect. One of our sergeants responded out to the registered address and advised that the vehicle that I located did not have the white bumper sticker. Upon closer inspection of the vehicle, the sergeant could see where a bumper sticker had recently been removed from the vehicle.

The next day, I was going on a week-long vacation, so I didn't get a chance to work the case any further. The rest of the unit set up surveillance on that same vehicle. I received a call in the north Georgia mountains thanking me and telling me about how much fun the surveillance of that suspect vehicle was and that the unit was able to arrest the black male suspect after he committed an armed robbery to a Dunkin Donut coffee shop in the county. That ended the robbery pattern.

***

We were contacted by detectives in the Sex Crimes Unit to provide information about a suspect that was exposing himself to women. The suspect was listed in a couple prior reports as being in the area with his maroon Nissan Frontier truck, but none of the victims had specifically identified him.

We responded out to the suspect's residence, where he lived with his parents. As soon as I drove past the front, the suspect was riding out of the alley on a bicycle. The previous incidents were occurring at a city park, where women would frequently be exercising. We conducted surveillance on the suspect and he rode directly to the same city park. The first night there were not any incidents.

On the second night, the suspect had driven his truck to the same park. The suspect had walked into the park in an area with some trees and benches and we lost sight of him. A couple minutes later, one of our detectives thought he could see him wearing "all light tan clothing" and sitting on a bench. About fifteen minutes later, the suspect came out of that area wearing dark shorts and a medium colored shirt. We assumed for a brief period that the suspect had been sitting on the city park bench totally naked, but were not certain.

We never were able to continue working the suspect. We were pulled to work a homicide case, which was of higher priority. When we were going to return to work the suspect, we found that he had moved to another city.

***

We worked another unusual request from the sex crimes unit. There were several reports that were taken by patrol officers where someone kept throwing pornographic magazines and videos along a certain couple block area. The area happened to be the same location of one of the largest bus stops for students. We set up in the area at 0500 hours, but none of us held much hope that we would see anyone throwing pornography at that time.

I was located in a slightly wooded area on foot slightly off the sidewalk, when I could observe a bicycle coming from the north. I notified other units that someone was in the area. I could not believe my ears, because I started to hear a sound similar to magazines hitting the ground as he rode closer. The suspect rode past my location and I was able to confirm that he was indeed discarding pornography along the sidewalk. I confirmed the offense to other detectives in the unit and they were able to arrest him without incident. We later learned that the suspect was a little mentally challenged (surprise) and he was dumpster diving at a local adult video store early in the morning. I later went to the store and spoke with the manager about putting a lock onto their dumpster.

***

There were numerous commercial burglary patterns that our unit worked. On one of the patterns, I was assigned to watch a large strip plaza. On the second night, I observed a white male with a cast on his arm acting suspicious up in the strip plaza. I started surveillance of the white male and requested other detectives to respond to assist me. After about fifteen minutes, another detective advised that he did not think that the white male was a good suspect to watch, so we all went back to our assigned positions.

The next night, I was sitting watching the strip plaza and I observed a 50 year old white male that was extremely intoxicated walk onto the property. The white male continued walking along the front of the businesses and eventually fell down. The white male crawled for about ten feet and then decided to simply sleep on the sidewalk. I advised other detectives of what I was watching and drove up to speak with the white male. I asked the white male if he needed any help and he replied no, so I went back to my position. I knew that I could simply watch him from my position and he could sleep off his intoxication.

After about thirty minutes, I observed what I initially thought was a black female walking along the street. The individual ended up being a male prostitute that had breast enhancements. Initially, the black male prostitute passed my position, but then I saw that he started looking at the white male up against the businesses.

At the moment this was happening, another one of our detectives observed the original young white male with the cast on his arm. The individual was acting suspicious again, so the remainder of the unit started surveillance on him.

I called for a uniformed patrol officer to respond to prevent the black male from taking property from the intoxicated white male. As the black male was getting closer to the intoxicated white male, I realized that the uniformed patrol officer was not going to make it in time to stop him. I pulled my vehicle from my position and could see the black male starting to do something to the white male. As I started into the parking lot, I observed the white male's bare buttocks shoot up into the air and it appeared that there was a struggle. I stopped a few feet away with my headlights shining on the two.

I stepped from my vehicle and approached. I was shocked to see that the black subject was indeed a male. The black male stated, "I am trying to help him and then stated I think he has rolled over on his glasses". The uniformed officer arrived as well as a rescue unit to check on the intoxicated white male. Initially, I placed the black male into the rear of the cruiser and had the uniformed officer obtain his information and run him for warrants.

I walked over to watch as rescue units rolled the intoxicated white male onto his stomach. The white male had a pair of prescription eyeglasses sitting on his buttocks with one earpiece broken off and one stuck into his anus. When this was mentioned to the intoxicated white male he reached around and pulled them out of his anus. I walked back over to the black male and placed him under arrest for sexual battery.

The black male spent nine months in jail and the State was having trouble getting cooperation from the victim. I am pretty certain he was too embarrassed to come into the courtroom and testify to anything that had happened to him. The case was dropped by the State and the black male was released from jail.

During my arrest, the remainder of my unit ended up following the white male with the cast on his arm and

arrested him when he broke the front glass to a
restaurant and ended the commercial burglary pattern.

Chapter 19

Sergeant M was a great sergeant for the unit, but that doesn't mean that we didn't have different opinions on occasion. He had previously been a detective in the unit before eventually becoming the sergeant, so he knew that the sergeant could not control everything. Every position in a surveillance held specific responsibilities and it didn't require a sergeant to direct detectives to do their job. Obviously, the sergeant did have his role in the unit, but many times on the street he was simply one of the units in the surveillance. If an individual detective could not work both with the group and independently, then they did not belong in the unit.

There are so many things that are unpredictable about police work and taking someone down in an arrest is certainly one of those areas. You never know how someone will react when they are cornered. There are certain approaches that officers can take and look to eliminate every obvious area for escape. Some individuals like to pretend that arresting someone is an exact science, but I used to always refer to arrest takedowns as "organized chaos". This name was coined because we may have responsibilities, but they all change based on the reactions of the suspect.

Since we all worked in an undercover capacity and drove undercover vehicles, we were also potential victims while we were on the street. There were numerous times that we would be parked on surveillance and a vehicle burglary suspect would come up and try to break into our vehicle. One time two of our detectives were together in a vehicle and a call came in to the communications center that a group of subjects were about to "rob them". We actually arrested a suspect after he approached. Another time, a suspect approached Sergeant M's vehicle and stole the valve stem caps off of his four tires. We made numerous arrests for the burglary attempts.

Sometimes it would be a gamble whether you could get help or trust a neighbor or other citizens. I used to talk with many neighbors of wanted suspects with hopes that they would call me information or the suspect's location in the future. One time we started working a 40 year old white male suspect that had defrauded several elderly victims and then battered one of them. The suspect lived on and off with his parents and we knew the location of their residence. I responded out to the location and spoke with some of the neighbors. I used to try to judge how much help a neighbor may be before I would even identify myself as a police officer.

I knocked on the door of a house right next door and a 60 year old white female answered the door. Her home looked very well maintained and appeared clean from the doorway. I asked her if she knew her neighbors to the right and without hesitation she started into a five minute rant about how much she hated them. The female continued to tell me about each of the three sons of the family and how they were all criminals. I identified myself as an officer and explained to her which son was wanted and what he was wanted for. I left a business card with the female, and she advised that she would call me as soon as she saw my suspect.

Two hours later, I answered my cell phone and it was the mother of my suspect calling. The mother advised that her neighbor came over and gave her my business card and she wanted to know what I wanted with her son. We ended up arresting him later without anyone's help.

***

Since we were undercover, we would also see things on the street that a uniformed officer would not get the chance to see. One day, I was simply driving up a busy street and I observed a vehicle stopped on one of the cross streets. The vehicle door opened as another black male approached and I could see the front seat passenger showing off an AR-15 rifle. I called for other detectives to assist me and we conducted surveillance of the vehicle. The vehicle ended up pulling into the driveway of a known residence, where a couple young felons lived.

We had uniformed officers stop the individuals before they went into the residence. All of the subjects denied having a rifle in the vehicle. The tint was so dark that you could not see inside the vehicle. Eventually, the car was unlocked and the AR-15 rifle was recovered and taken off the street.

***

One late evening shift, I was working on foot in a residential neighborhood. I had started to move down an alley to make it to the next block. I could see a man sitting on his rear porch, get up, go inside his residence, and come back outside with a handgun. The man was looking in my direction, but was about 35 yards away from me. I yelled to the man, "Sir, I am a police officer, take your gun back inside." Luckily, that was enough, because the man did go inside his residence and I continued through the alley.

***

We tried to get as much help from citizens as we were able to get. One time, we were looking for a suspect for active warrants and were able to speak with a known acquaintance of his. The acquaintance advised that he could call us later and let us know of the suspect's location. The acquaintance advised further that we should use caution because the suspect always carried three guns everywhere that he went. Now, this sounded like some tall tale, but we approached every suspect as if they were armed.

The acquaintance called later with the hotel and room number of where the suspect was staying. We set

171

up surveillance on the room and observed the suspect walking away from it. We moved in to affect the arrest and the suspect ran across a six lane roadway and was eventually taken to the ground in the parking lot of a McDonald's restaurant. After the suspect was handcuffed, we were shocked to find three separate handguns on the suspect.

***

I also used my undercover position as an opportunity to yell things at uniformed officers or ask them ridiculous questions in front of citizens, who did not know I was also a police officer. Detective W and I were driving around the downtown area late one evening shift. I observed Officer M standing on the City sidewalk surrounded by a group of citizens while he was working off-duty at a bar. I slowed the vehicle and yelled, "Hey officer thanks for saving my life!" Without hesitation, Officer M looks at me in the face and states, "Ha! Blow me." We continued driving, so I didn't get to see the reaction from the citizens. The only thing that I truly missed in the undercover unit was the comradery that I used to enjoy with everyone around the police station.

***

Our evening shift squad was constantly being pulled to work dayshift for various residential burglary patterns. I never minded changing shifts as long as there was a true need for the additional manpower. Whenever evening shift would change shifts, it would throw us out of our routine for the entire week both on the job and at home. Sergeant M had moved back to a patrol position, so we had a second new sergeant in the unit. Both of the "new" sergeants had over 25 years on the department, but they were new to the unit. Sometimes the new sergeants in the unit would simply rely on information provided from burglary detectives or other details about a pattern that was a bit exaggerated.

172

The entire unit was working a very strong daytime burglary pattern. The suspects were believed to be juveniles that would either approach in a stolen car, on foot, or on bicycles. I had observed a group of four black males that were riding through the area that I was watching. I moved my position and observed them ride westbound into an alley. I called for additional detectives to move into the area to assist on surveillance.

Once other units were set up in the area, I decided to walk through the alley to ensure that the suspects were not committing a burglary. About half way down the alley, I observed one of the individuals acting as a lookout at the alley side of the property. As I approached I simply stated, "What's up man" and I continued walking past him westbound. I had looked over his shoulder and observed the three other suspects up to a window on the south side of a residence prying it open. I notified other units over the radio of what I had observed and to move in to affect an arrest.

I was holding in a position to the west and I observed the suspects attempting to flee in a southbound direction on their bicycles. All of the detectives on the operation, uniformed officers, and K-9 officers moved in to take the suspects into custody. All four suspects were arrested and charged with the burglary.

***

We were notified by patrol officers that they had observed a stolen blue Ford F-250 in a certain area of the City. Our unit responded to the area and we were able to locate the truck driving around, so we started surveillance of the vehicle. We continued surveillance of the vehicle for almost an hour before the suspects realized that we were watching them. After that the suspects continued driving, but were looking for a place that they could escape from us.

At one point, they drove down a street in a different jurisdiction that was a dead end. Detective S and I had followed them partially down the dead end roadway and stopped along the side of the road when we saw the suspect headed back in the opposite direction. The driver intentionally swerved the stolen truck at my undercover vehicle and then did the same to Detective S. The suspect vehicle actually knocked the mirror of Detective S's vehicle.

The vehicle started driving to different parts of our City at high rates of speed and was still hoping to lose our undercover vehicles. We obtained the assistance of the county's helicopter to ensure that we did not lose the vehicle. I had one of the oldest vehicles in the unit, which was a 1988 Ford Bronco. The pursuit proved to be too much for the aging vehicle and it started to billow black smoke from the rear as I continued to chase the stolen truck. Both the helicopter and Sergeant M advised me that my vehicle was literally on fire. I ended up calling uniformed Officer B on his cell phone and asked him to meet me at a nearby park. I parked my undercover vehicle and jumped into Officer B's marked cruiser, so I wouldn't miss out on the arrest.

Chief of Police H had been listening to the pursuit for almost an hour and finally advised our units that we had authorization to box the vehicle in as soon as an opportunity arose. The vehicle drove through an alley and we boxed the stolen truck within that alley. All three suspects were taken into custody without incident. The driver was charged with the stolen vehicle, fleeing and eluding, and two counts of aggravated assault against law enforcement.

The case went to "trial" in juvenile court. At that time, there was an extremely liberal judge assigned to the juvenile division named Judge S. The initial statement from Judge S was, "Okay, Suspect L I see that you are in a program for (insert previous crimes here), how is that program going for you?" Had I crossed over into a different reality? Suspect L was standing before her with the new charges of auto theft, fleeing and eluding, and two counts of aggravated assault against two police officers, of course the program was not working for him. Even the citizen victims sitting in the courtroom saw that juvenile court was a complete waste of time.

The juvenile circus continued for another forty minutes and Judge S decided to leave Suspect L in the same program, but mandated that he apologized to the victims in the courtroom. This silly act only further enraged the citizen victims.

***

We obtained information from homicide detectives that they had developed probable cause for homicide for the arrest of a black male suspect. The full description of the suspect, pictures from prior arrests, and a known address where he was supposed to be staying were provided to our unit. The detectives advised further that the suspect was making plans to leave for Texas on that same day. We went out to the location to set up surveillance.

As soon as Detective N arrived at the location, he observed a black male that fit the physical description of our suspect run from the residence and jump into the front passenger seat of a black 1998 Chrysler Sebring. Another black male was driving the vehicle and it quickly pulled away from the residence. The vehicle drove directly to the interstate and started to head northbound. We attempted to have one of our uniformed patrol officers in place to stop the vehicle, but no units were available.

The vehicle drove across a seven mile bridge into the jurisdiction of another city. We attempted to contact that city's police department, but the vehicle had driven into the county's jurisdiction before we could get some assistance. Finally, we notified the county and they had units in route. One of the troopers from the Florida Highway Patrol was monitoring the county's radio channel and was in the area. The trooper arrived on scene and initiated a traffic stop, but the vehicle started to flee from the cruiser.

The information about the potential homicide suspect had been communicated to the communications center of the county and to the Florida Highway Patrol communications. However, the information that they received was that we had already confirmed the identity of the subject and he was indeed our suspect. The Florida Highway Patrol authorized a pursuit of the vehicle. Luckily, the trooper knew how to drive, because the suspect vehicle fled at over 100 miles per hour at times.

As the pursuit continued, it drew the attention of a couple of Florida Department of transportation cruisers, and a few of the sheriff's deputies from the county. The pursuit continued into another county and ended up picking up a couple of sheriff's deputies from that county and the Florida Highway Patrol airplane. The pursuit continued to just inside another county and the suspect vehicle decided to get off of the interstate. The area that the suspect exited was very rural and none of our detectives knew where they were going, but the pursuit continued. At one point, I was stuck simply moving in the direction of the FHP airplane, because I lost radio connections.

The suspect drove off of the paved roadway and tried to elude the trooper and other cruisers by driving through a big field. Detective N drove through the field a couple minutes later and ended up speaking to a farmer (you can't make this stuff up). Detective N asked, "Did you see a black car drive through here?" The farmer replied, "You bet I did and that trooper was right on his ass!"

Eventually, there were so many cruisers and the suspect really did not have a plan of escape. The suspect vehicle ended up driving into a ditch and both of the subjects were taken into custody. All of our detectives from the unit were still trying to locate the arrest scene. I ended up being the first detective from our unit to arrive and I had a picture and the information of the wanted suspect.

As soon as I walked up to the cruiser that held the front seat passenger, I stated, "That is not our guy." In desperation the Sergeant from the Florida Highway Patrol held my photograph next to the arrested subject and stated, "I think that it looks like him." There was going to be a whole lot of paperwork to document a whole lot of nothing. The black male driver advised that he fled from police simply because he did not have a driver's license. The front seat passenger was a juvenile and ended up being released to a guardian at the arrest scene.

***

We were contacted by our Homicide and Robbery units to assist them in arresting a homicide suspect, Suspect M. Earlier on that same day, Suspect M committed a robbery to a small local convenience store located in the neighborhood. During the robbery, Suspect M had the Indian male store clerk down on his knees pleading for his life and he shot the victim in the head execution style.

Next, the robbery was interrupted by a customer, simply walking in –the wrong place at the wrong time- and he was shot and killed inside the store. Suspect M then thought he removed the store surveillance system tape and took it with him. Prior to getting out of the exit another customer stepped inside. Suspect M did not hesitate, but when he raised the gun it malfunctioned. Suspect M fixed the gun and shot the third victim in the face, but that victim would survive.

We were showed the surveillance video from the cameras in the store. We had all of the information on Suspect M and set up surveillance on his residence. The residence was a two story half address that sat right off the alley. Detective L and I were positioned on foot near the property. After a couple of hours, we observed some activity at that residence. We observed two black males come down the exterior stairwell and walk out into the alley. We were able to positively confirm the identity of Suspect M and we advised other units over the radio. When they were about a half block away from the residence, many units moved in to arrest the two and Suspect M was taken into custody without incident.

Suspect M had his trial and was convicted five years later. The judge sentenced Suspect M to two separate death sentences.

***

We were contacted by the sex crimes unit to assist them in working surveillance on a subject that was "peeping" into residences. The uniformed patrol officers had identified Suspect D's vehicle in the area after a recent complaint of a "peeping". Suspect D was a 40 year old black male and did not live anywhere close to the neighborhood where the complaints were coming from.

We set up the surveillance on Suspect D's residence and the vehicle was parked right out front. Suspect D drove a full size maroon and silver Ford Econoline van. On the first night, Suspect D left his residence and drove straight to the Dairy Queen and it required him to drive through the target area where the "peeping" incidents were happening. We initially thought maybe he worked at the Dairy Queen and he possibly committed the "peeping" incidents on his way to work.

Sergeant M advised that he needed a volunteer to go inside the Dairy Queen and see if Suspect D was an employee. I was very quick to seize this responsibility and to blend in with other customers I planned to purchase a medium sized Reese's Cup blizzard. I entered the Dairy Queen and the blizzard plan worked perfectly. I was able to determine that Suspect D was sitting and waiting like he was picking someone up and we later determined that his son worked at the Dairy Queen.

On the next night, Suspect D left his residence a few minutes earlier and our surveillance led us to the target neighborhood for the "peeping". We watched as Suspect D was "peeping" into three or four victim's windows within the neighborhood. Suspect D was placed under arrest by uniformed officers. We spoke with the different victims and one of the victims advised that she breastfed her child in the room that Suspect D was "peeping".

***

We had another "peeping" suspect a few years later in a different neighborhood. On this "peeping" pattern, we did not know who our suspect was from the start. We set up surveillance in the area and were drawn quickly to watching a subject that was riding around the neighborhood on a bicycle. This individual was a 40 year old white male named Suspect M and he lived in the neighborhood. We started surveillance on Suspect M and it wasn't long before he was up to a residence "peeping". Upon the arrest of Suspect M, he claimed in defense that all of the residents "like it" when he looked into their windows.

Chapter 20

We started working a case to locate a wanted suspect after a recent bank robbery. The suspect was wanted specifically for the bank robbery and also had active arrest warrants for other crimes. The information was sent to us after an investigation by the robbery unit. The robbery detectives advised that the suspect was a crack addict, had become very paranoid, and always carried a handgun down the front of his pants. Many times detectives will have heard "through the grape vine" that suspects had bragged about not being taken alive by police and this suspect had stated this claim to someone.

We had tracked the suspect to staying in an apartment room on the second level of an old warehouse. The warehouse was just outside the jurisdiction of the City, but was still within the same county. The warehouse was surrounded by a six foot privacy fence with barbed wire and had openings at each end of the building. We set up with half the unit inside the fence and half outside and started the surveillance. At the time we started surveillance, we did not know if the suspect was inside the apartment or not.

I was partnered with Detective N at the time and we were set up to the east. We observed a white male come down from the apartment and walk outside talking on his cell phone. We were able to confirm by looking at the white male that it was indeed our suspect. We instructed Detectives C and J to move in from the west inside the warehouse to take the suspect down as he went back into the building. We were going to cover the east end of the building, if the suspect started to run out on foot.

The suspect finished his phone call and walked back into the warehouse, so we started to approach on foot. Detective N and I were coming up from the southeast.

From our angle we could still see the suspect and we heard Detectives C and J challenging him to put his hands into the air. We watched as the suspect raised both of his hands and stopped walking. It initially appeared that the suspect was going to give up peacefully. Originally, I had my issued Glock semi-automatic handgun in my hand, but at this point I was switching to utilize my Taser. Detective N and I were going to stay together and he would cover both of us with his firearm, if needed. It appeared that the suspect was giving up and following commands.

I took my eyes off of the suspect for a split second and heard gunfire. I looked back to the suspect and could see that his hands were lowered and heard a few more rounds of fire. From out of our sight, Detective J had fired six rounds from an AR-15 rifle at the suspect. I quickly switched back to my handgun and approached the suspect. The suspect had fallen to the floor of the warehouse, but was still moving his arms and legs. I challenged the suspect to keep his hands visible, as Detective S handcuffed him. I holstered my handgun and assisted Detective S in searching the suspect. The suspect was not armed, but had pretended to pull a gun on Detective J to commit "suicide by cop". Rescue units were called to the scene to treat the suspect.

I could see that the suspect was visibly in pain, but was not speaking and having trouble breathing. The suspect had been struck once in the left hip and at least twice in the chest, probably through both lungs. The suspect was grasping onto our pant legs for help and I told the suspect to concentrate on his breathing. The rescue units knew that the suspect was a trauma alert for the emergency room and had scheduled for helicopter transportation from a nearby location. The suspect was transported from the scene to the helicopter and escorted by a uniformed officer. We also had to notify the sheriff's department for the county that we had a shooting in their jurisdiction.

At the shooting scene, one of the robbery detectives told me that the suspect had passed away. I asked the detective, "Are you certain that the suspect is dead?" and they advised, "Yes, he is definitely dead." Just like with a death notification to a family, I wanted to be certain that the information was true. That information was a little premature. The union attorney was Attorney C and he arrived on scene. I initially briefed Attorney C on everything that had occurred, including telling him that the suspect was deceased.

Next, Attorney C spoke with Detective J about what had occurred and Attorney C informed Detective J that the suspect was deceased. Attorney C then had Detective J call his family and talk to them. Attorney C and I learned together that the suspect had not died and was simply too unstable to transport by helicopter. Detective J called his family back to advise them that the suspect had not died. Of course, since everything plays out as it happens, the suspect died on the way to the hospital. Detective J called his family once again to advise them that the suspect was, "really dead this time".

The shooting occurred outside the City's jurisdiction, so the deputies in the county investigated it. When there is an officer involved shooting, there are several investigations that occur sometimes simultaneously. The first is a criminal investigation by the police agency that has jurisdiction. This criminal investigation is closely followed by and presented to the State Attorney's Office for their investigation, and they make the determination on any charges being filed. The last investigation is completed by the internal affairs division of the shooting officer's agency. The internal affairs investigation is not as pressing to be completed as quickly and can sometimes be spread over several weeks. Of course, the court of public opinion begins investigating the shooting immediately without any verifiable facts.

We all had to respond to the county's Sheriff's Office and were independently interviewed just like any other witness would be. After that was completed, we also had to provide testimony to a state attorney, who was called in specifically for this shooting. We all worked that night until about 0700 hours, but each and every officer went home.

***

We were working a creep-in burglary pattern, but did not have a suspect identified. We watched the activity of the area, which was a heavily residential area of seven blocks that sat between two major streets. The neighborhood was used by many simply as a cut-through to go from one main street to the other.

We started watching a 50 year old white male that appeared to be transient. The suspect had been walking aimlessly through the neighborhood and had also walked behind some houses where there wasn't an alley. The white male finally chose his target house and went to the rear of the residence. Our unit was set up around the residence as the suspect took off a screen and entered the home.

Sergeant M decided that he wanted one of our detectives to knock on the door to either scare the suspect to leave or to get the resident victims out of any danger. The funny part of the whole scenario was the fact that Sergeant M asked Detective P to accomplish this task. The neighborhood was full of primarily white residents, it was after midnight, and Detective P was a black male.

Detective P rang the doorbell and a 60 year old white female answered the door. Detective P attempted to state to the female in a very low voice that he was a police officer and he needed her out of the residence because there was a suspect inside. I am pretty sure that all the white female heard was "I am a black man and it is after midnight".

Detective P looked over the white female's shoulder and could see the suspect crouched down against the rear wall. Detective P grabbed ahold of the female and pulled her out of the residence to safety. The female screamed for about a whole minute. The suspect observed this and jumped right out the rear window that he had come in through. The suspect was taken into custody without incident.

***

We worked a pattern on the evening shift of suspects stealing bicycles in the downtown area. We started surveillance of a black male that was walking around with a backpack. The suspect was observed going up to a bicycle rack, cutting a chain, and leaving on a bicycle. We continued surveillance until we had everyone in a position for a takedown.

The suspect was riding southbound on the east sidewalk of a street. I was walking northbound on that same sidewalk. The suspect could see me walking toward him on the west edge of that same sidewalk, so he moved to the east edge of the sidewalk. The suspect was getting closer, so moved to the east edge of that sidewalk. The suspect quickly attempted to move back to the west edge of the sidewalk and I stepped right in front of his bicycle. The suspect stopped abruptly and I grabbed the handlebars of the bicycle and stated, "You know what time it is?" I had heard that line used in actual robberies as well as in jokes about robberies and I finally was able to use it.

The suspect looked me right in the eyes and jumped backward falling to the asphalt street. I laid the bicycle on its' side and moved toward the suspect. The suspect looked like he wanted to run, but three of us grabbed ahold of him and placed him into handcuffs.

We were working an evening shift, when we heard a call of a hit and run to a bicycle with injuries dispatched. We were not too far away, so our unit moved to the area. We could see what looked to be a trail of fluids that lead in a basic northbound direction. As I continued to follow the trail of fluids, we were advised that the bicyclist was confirmed deceased by rescue units.

I came to a location where there was something in the roadway, so I stopped my undercover vehicle to get out and investigate. I could see a larger puddle of fluids in the road and then identified the object in the roadway as the lower leg of the deceased. It was basically the leg of the victim that had been ripped off below the knee and it still had a shoe on the foot.

I looked to the east and could see a vehicle parked on the north side of a Red Lobster restaurant and I knew that the business was closed. I approached on foot to investigate. I could still hear two other detectives in my unit following the trail of fluid northbound. I approached a Hispanic male with a maroon minivan. The subject advised that he was driving along and ran over a bicycle that was lying on the roadway in front of the Red Lobster restaurant. The subject advised further that the impact punctured his oil pan, so he was waiting for a ride. The subject had taken the bicycle and put it into the rear of his minivan to dispose of it later. I informed the subject about the hit and run fatality and the fact that I needed to take custody of the bicycle for evidence.

About that time, other detectives had caught up with the suspect vehicle and followed him right to his residence. The suspect was taken into custody as he exited the vehicle and was found to be intoxicated. Uniformed officers responded to the scene, took custody of the bicycle, and secured the scene around the leg in the roadway.

***

We were provided information from the robbery unit of a robbery pattern that was occurring in three counties. We were provided the name of the black male suspect, Suspect R, who lived in another county. We started surveillance on that suspect.

Suspect R lived about 45 miles from our headquarters, so we were driving many miles all week long. On about the second night, Suspect R left his residence just as the first detective was arriving, so the remainder of the unit was trying to play catch up in the surveillance. Suspect R drove about 40 miles from his residence to a 7-11 that was inside another county. Suspect R parked his vehicle north and west of that 7-11 and approached on foot.

We were all set up to observe the robbery and as an arrest team for after the robbery occurred. We waited for about 40 minutes, but I guess the store was too busy. Suspect R simply left his hiding spot on the side of the 7-11 and went back to his vehicle. Every night, Suspect R drove a minimum of 150 miles, which meant we were driving well over 200 miles per night.

Finally, Suspect R ended up going to a Circle K gas station that was in our county, but still outside the jurisdiction of our City. We set up around the store. Suspect R actually parked right next to Detectives P and O, who were in their undercover vehicle. Suspect R exited his vehicle and tried to look into their undercover vehicle to convince himself that it was empty.

Suspect R walked about a block to the east side of the parking lot. As luck would have it, a uniformed police officer from that city's jurisdiction pulled onto the parking lot and the officer went into the store. Suspect R stood up and ran back to his vehicle. Suspect R drove around for about fifteen minutes and then returned to the Circle K gas station. This time Suspect R parked a little closer to the store.

Suspect R approached on foot as he had done before, but this time went right up to the front and inside to commit the armed robbery. We were set up to take the suspect down as he fled from the store. Suspect R came running out of the store northbound as two customers approached the store from the west. Suspect R was challenged by a group of detectives, but quickly changed his course and jumped over a six foot privacy fence continuing northbound. Suspect R then ran to the east around a very tall warehouse building and we would discover later that he threw his firearm up on top of this building.

Detective L challenged Suspect R again and he jumped a fence into an old maintenance yard to a marine storage facility. The entire yard was filled with old cars, trailers, and boats. Suspect R was eventually located inside the yard and taken into custody.

The robbery detectives compiled all of their cases from the three counties and charged Suspect R with as many of the offenses as they could. Months later, the State Attorney's Office came to our office to meet with us to ensure that everyone had all of the facts of the cases in order. We had all received our subpoenas and were all prepared to go to trial on Suspect R. The morning that the trial was supposed to start, I heard on the local news update over the radio as I driving to work, that Suspect R had committed suicide in the jail. Initially, no one believed me when I arrived at work, because I was always full of it.

Chapter 21

We were working a case of a group of suspects that had possibly been identified in a pattern of robberies to drug stores, such as CVS and Walgreens. There were four to five white males in their late teens and early twenties and one black male about 18 years old identified from the group. We started working surveillance on them every evening. On about the third night, the group was at a nearby bowling alley. At the time, no one in our surveillance unit knew what lay in store for us that evening.

After a couple of hours, one of the white males, Suspect M, drove to Suspect K's residence, who was a known 18 year old white female that lived with her parents. Suspect M met up with the black male, Suspect H. The two left in Suspect M's vehicle and drove to an apartment complex across town. I observed Suspect M go up to the second floor apartment wearing lighter clothing and then return to the vehicle wearing all black clothing. This fact would later become problematic to get into the courtroom.

The two left this apartment and returned to Suspect K's house. After just a couple minutes, a 2001, silver Volkswagen Jetta left the residence quickly, but we did not know who was inside the vehicle. During the surveillance of this vehicle, we were able to determine that Suspect K was driving and both Suspect M and Suspect H were inside the vehicle. The group went to a nearby gas station, purchased some gas, and then continued driving westbound. They drove to an intersection of two busy streets, which had a CVS on the southeast corner. We believed that the CVS had closed at 2200 hours, so we were not certain where the group was headed.

They turned southbound and drove three blocks and then turned westbound. They drove through a parking lot of a Blockbuster Video store and continued to circulate on the west side of that main roadway. We thought that they were possibly going to make an attempt at the CVS and find it closed or they were looking for a get-away location for a robbery that would occur on a future date. Ten minutes passed and their vehicle had been circulating a few minutes and then parked for a few minutes, all within the couple blocks west of that main roadway.

After sitting parked for a couple more minutes, the vehicle traveled eastbound on the avenue that ran along the south side of the Blockbuster Video store. They were headed toward the main roadway and initially, it appeared like maybe they were leaving the area. The vehicle stopped abruptly and the two male suspects jumped out with shirts around their heads. Detective P advised that they were running up toward the west doors of the Blockbuster Video store with guns in their hands. The suspect vehicle continued eastbound and turned south onto the main roadway.

Suspect M and Suspect H ran into the Blockbuster Video pointing guns at the two female clerks who were working inside. We had to scramble to organize our takedown of the suspects for when they came back out the west doors. I had previously dropped my partner, Detective L, off on foot to the west of the Blockbuster Video store. I was parked behind a plaza of stores to the south of the Blockbuster Video store, so I left my vehicle there and approached on foot.

Detective N pulled his truck onto the southwest corner of the parking lot to use as cover and Detectives F, T, and N all stood behind it. Detective L had taken a position behind the only citizen vehicle on the parking lot to the west and was advising what he could see inside the business. Detective P and I took a position on the south side of the business at the southwest corner. Detective S and Sergeant M followed Suspect K as she drove to a get-away position to the southwest.

They were able to arrest Suspect K, when she stopped behind the businesses to the south right next to where I parked my vehicle.

From my position, I could look north along the masonry wall of Blockbuster Video and see the west exit doors, but could not see anything inside. I had already envisioned the suspects coming outside and knew that I did not want to stand right at the corner because ricochet rounds would ride along the masonry wall to my position. Detective P and I were speaking briefly with each other. When you are waiting for suspects to complete their crimes, seconds pass like minutes.

Detective L advised over the radio that the suspects had their guns pointed at the two females and that they were at the registers. All of the other detectives were only about 20 yards to the west from my position, so we could also speak with each other without the radio. At one point, Detective L held up his right forearm to his neck to mimic a hostage hold to me. Detective L advised that they were moving away from the registers further inside the store and he observed the suspects move to the south in the store out of sight. Detective L stated that he could not see anyone inside the store anymore.

We were all standing right there with our guns in our hands and I knew that someone needed to move up and see what was going on inside the store. There was no other way to prevent or ensure that a sexual assault or murder was not about to happen. I knew that I would be fully exposed by putting myself in front of the west windows and doors. There was a single door, emergency exit, on the east side of that south wall with a ramp that led down to the avenue to the south. I turned to Detective P and stated, "Watch that door!" and ran up toward the windows and exit door on the west side of the business. That simple statement would haunt me for years.

As I approached the glass, I could not see anyone inside the business and assumed that if the suspects came out the doors, we would be shooting at each other from very close range. I was about to state on the radio that I could not see anyone inside the store, when gunfire erupts from the south. I ran back southbound along the west side of the business and heard about a full second pause in the shots being fired just before I ran around the corner.

Once I cleared the corner, I could see the back of Detective P as he was kneeling on his right knee and facing east, and I observed Detective P fire two rounds at Suspect M. I could see Suspect M was already falling to the ground toward the east facing away from me and observed his body actually flop as it hit the ground. Over the top of Detective P's head I could also see Suspect H who was running at a full sprint southbound across the avenue. I simply continued in my run, as I passed Detective P to pursue Suspect H on foot.

All of my other partners had also started running toward the shooting and the suspects. We chased Suspect H southbound for one full block and he was taken to the ground on the south side of the next avenue. Suspect H had dropped his gun approximately twenty feet from where we took him to the ground. I handcuffed Suspect H with the assistance of the detectives that had taken him to the ground.

I had the front of my right shin resting on top of Suspect H's shoulder blade as he lay on the ground. For a split second, we were all happy to know that all three suspects were "in custody". I had assumed at that moment that Suspect M was deceased the way I observed him flop to the ground. I immediately keyed up my radio and stated, "Detective P are you ten-four." There was no response, so I again stated, "Detective P are you ten-four." I yelled to detectives F, T, and L to run back and check on Detective P, because we still were not getting any response over the radio. Within a few seconds, I heard "officer down" come over the radio, after they ran the single block back to the shooting scene.

I was "stuck" with the prisoner, Suspect H, but knew everything was being done for Detective P. I simply kept Suspect H handcuffed on the ground, since I was by myself and had the suspect's firearm on scene twenty feet away. I thought about the fact that I had observed Detective P make those last two shots at Suspect M and had no idea that he had been injured or possibly shot. Unfortunately, it was the latter and Detective P was shot in the forearm and in the left lower abdomen. Detective P was the only detective that returned fire.

I knew that uniformed officers had already been called to our scene from our City. The robbery played out eleven blocks outside of our City, but was still inside the county that we worked. Uniformed officer, Officer C, arrived to assist me. We stood Suspect H up, completed the search, and placed him into Officer C's marked cruiser. We took his gloves and the shirt around his neck as evidence. I asked Officer C to stand by the firearm at the arrest scene until another uniformed officer arrived to take custody of that scene. I was finally able to return to the shooting scene to hear the status of Detective P.

I jogged through the one block parking lot up to the shooting scene, but unfortunately, I stumbled upon a dark colored nylon bag lying flat against the asphalt of the parking lot. I looked inside the bag without disturbing its' position and discovered that it had U.S. currency. This bag contained the money taken in the robbery, so I stood by with the bag for approximately two minutes until I was able to have Sergeant K take my position and watch the evidence.

Again, finally, I had the chance to go and check on my injured friend, Detective P. Although my time had been occupied, I was able to observe from a distance all of the rescue personnel and deputies from the county that were at the shooting scene. As I made it back to the scene, the ambulance with Detective P inside was leaving and headed to the trauma hospital. I learned that Suspect M was only hit with a round in the hip and was very much alive. Suspect M was also taken to the hospital and days later taken to jail.

I was just starting to hear some detailed information on Detective P, when three drunk white males came walking up from the east. One of the males says to me, "Hey, officer, if you need any witnesses, we saw everything." I asked the subject, "Okay, sir, what did you see?" The subject advised that they were all drinking at the bar on the east side of the busy roadway and they heard all of the gunfire. The subject continued to tell me that as soon as the shots sounded, that they all jumped onto the floor of the bar. I instructed the three subjects that they could return to the bar to drink and if deputies needed to ask them about what they had "seen" they would come over to get them.

For a short period, we were able to go to the hospital and we could see Detective P in surgery and also watch his status on a TV monitor across the hall. The Chief of Police and many others in the command staff arrived at the hospital, as well as the Mayor from the City. Everyone was pretty much helpless. It was extremely hard to go home after that long shift, because we knew that Detective P was not able to go to his home.

We all eventually went home, slept for a couple hours, and responded back to the hospital. Since the robbery occurred in another jurisdiction, the county deputies investigated the offense. Once again we responded to the Sheriff's Office for interviews by detectives and then interviews and testimony to the State Attorney's Office, which lasted for hours. The following week consisted of spending a little time at home and many long hours at the hospital. Detective P continued to improve and eventually returned to our unit after many long months of recovery.

My words to Detective P, prior to him getting shot, would seem pretty simple to anyone who was not on scene. I stated, "Watch that door!" In my mind, I was thinking watch out for that door, as being an access to the suspect's escape and they would have come out twenty feet behind Detective P, as he waited on that southwest corner with his back to the door. I knew I was leaving Detective P in that position alone, but thought that I was the one heading into the danger.

I wished I had stated, "Watch out for that door!" By not adding those two additional words, I believe my statement sent Detective P to that door at the exact moment the suspects were coming out. The difference may sound trivial, but Detective P would have been safer being further away from the door. Those were the thoughts that haunted me for years, because, like everyone else, the events of that evening played over and over in my head at various times.

Now, Detective P was a very capable detective. He had about five more years of experience in policing than I had at the time and two years longer in the Special Investigations Unit. I am not in any way questioning Detective P's abilities as an officer or his ability to make his own decisions. Although we all watch each other's backs, there is simply no way to control everything, especially a suspect's actions, and I know that. You don't have to work in policing very long to know that shit happens fast! Also, you learn that in high stress situations, you do what you do, and you don't get the luxury of pondering over options or playing out scenarios. Most important police decisions are made in less than a second.

About a year and a half later, the trial for Suspect M, the shooter, was set. We all had subpoenas and were set to testify. As an officer, I had already testified hundreds of times before the state attorney and numerous times in court, but this case was certainly different. There was a higher stress level that all of us were feeling as we waited to be called into the courtroom.

I was called into the court by the bailiff on duty. I entered the public courtroom that was only occupied by less than ten citizens, with several being Detective P's family. I was sworn in as usual and took my seat on the stand. In almost every criminal case, there are certain "truths" about what occurred in the offense that can't be spoken in the courtroom. In this trial, there were many motions prior to the trial, where rulings were made about what facts could be stated in court and which facts could not be spoken. One of those "truths" that we could not speak of was the fact that we were conducting surveillance on the suspects for the pattern of robberies. The "truths" could not be brought up by the prosecutor, but if the defense attorney asks the question, even one about the excluded information, that question can be answered with a truthful answer. This scenario is commonly referred to the defense "opening the door" to certain facts that would have been excluded from the courtroom.

The prosecutor on the case for the State Attorney's Office was very thorough and wanted the jury to know that I observed Suspect M change into his black robbery outfit prior to committing the robbery. This obviously would show the jury the premeditation that Suspect M had used. The prosecutor struggled with the exact question that she could ask me where I could provide testimony that would be acceptable to the court. Initially, I had to tell the prosecutor that I did not believe that I could answer her questions a couple of times. Then the prosecutor attempted a few more questions to get an answer from me and the defense objected to each question. After each attempted question, the judge would have to clear the jury out of the courtroom, so they did not hear any discussion about details that they were not authorized to hear.

The judge had already cleared the jury four times and thirty minutes passed before I had really testified to any details on the offense. Finally, the judge states, "You ladies come to an agreement on what you want this detective to say, and I will order him to say it." I was not comfortable with the judge's statement at all, for I was fully prepared to testify to the truth. I knew that the judge could not authorize me to perjure myself, no more than she could authorize me to commit any other crime. Luckily, the prosecutor and defense agreed to a series of questions that the state attorney would ask that would simply lead me to testify to the fact that early in the night I observed Suspect M in lighter clothing and that he changed into the black outfit right before the robbery. I was on the stand for ninety minutes to provide all of my actions and observations to the court, which should have taken only ten minutes.

All three of the suspects from that robbery were eventually convicted on that offense and two other males in their group were also convicted on previous drug store robberies for a total of five suspects sent to prison. Suspect M (the shooter) was sentenced to life in prison, Suspect H (robbery co-defendant) pled and was sentenced to 30 years in prison, and Suspect K (getaway driver) pled and was sentenced to 15 years in prison.

Chapter 22

Approximately nine months after Detective P was shot, we had to work through another tragic shooting. The evening shift started out like any other. We arrived at work, reviewed the previous day's reports, and went out to dinner. We usually rode together with our partners, unless we were working special cases that required us to ride separately. On this day, I was driving and I had my partner, Detective L, riding with me.

A couple of hours had passed since dinner and we were not working any specific case or looking for any specific suspect. I decided that I wanted to "make a run for coffee". Since Detective L advised that he did not want any coffee, I decided I would go to the Racetrack gas station and get a frozen coffee flavored drink. That simple decision would change our fates forever.

I traveled northbound on the main road that led to the Racetrack gas station. We were about twenty blocks away, when three black males crossed in front of us. The three were traveling westbound along the south sidewalk of a major avenue. Both Detective L and I looked at each other and stated, "We are watching them" in unison. We knew the three did not belong in the area and were exhibiting criminal behaviors. I parked briefly in a position northeast of them and we watched as they continued westbound. They continued for one and a half blocks and then cut southbound between two businesses. I drove around the perimeter of where we had last observed them and we could not find them again.

Next, I decided to actually drive westbound through the alley that they should have entered or crossed. I continued driving into the next block of that alley and we observed the three slightly separated as they stood in the west parking lot of a small pharmacy. The three looked at my undercover vehicle, but did not pay us too much attention, as I continued driving. I drove through that block of the alley to the street and let Detective L get out on foot to observe the suspects' actions. At this point, we thought the three were suspicious and called for the remainder of our unit to assist us in the surveillance.

Detective L advised that he could see all three of the suspects and after just a couple minutes they started to walk eastbound in the alley. The three suspects walked for a block and a half and Detective L was having a hard time seeing them, so I pulled my vehicle into the alley and began calling the suspects' actions. Detective S arrived in the area with his partner, Detective P, and they took a position to the east. The suspects continued for just over one block and then they disappeared off the alley to the north. After only seconds, the three came back into my view and into the alley with bicycles and they started riding westbound in that same alley. We were not certain if they had stolen the bicycles or had hidden their own bicycles earlier.

The three rode all the way back to the parking lot next to the pharmacy store and stopped. By this time, we had a total of five undercover vehicles that were watching the suspects' actions. My partner, Detective L, was still out on foot and was a block east of the suspects in the alley. I was parked mid-block on the avenue south of that alley. It was my responsibility to watch the back of Detective L as best as I could, by watching anyone moving into the area. I could not actually see Detective L, because he was north of a row of buildings. I could see Sergeant M on foot one block west, trying to look for the suspects through the buildings from the avenue south of them.

Detectives N and P had taken a position to the northwest and were also intermittently calling out the actions of the suspects. Initially, Detective S advised that there was a Dodge van parked on the avenue to the north and they may be looking to steal it. Later, Detective N advised that he thought that the group may be looking toward an Exxon gas station that was slightly northwest of the suspects' position. I called over the district patrol channel for uniformed officers to move into the area and monitor our radio channel.

Approximately one minute later, Detective N came across the police radio, "Alright, guys they are masked up and they are running toward the Exxon gas station." Detective N continued, "They are going to do a robbery." I grabbed my patrol radio and called out a robbery in progress and provided the location to all uniformed officers in the patrol district.

Detective N continued to call out the actions of the suspects as best as he could see inside the store. A decision was made to take down the suspects in the alley, where they left their bikes. I jumped out of my undercover vehicle as I was finishing notifying patrol officers of the robbery and ran west to the street. Some patrol officers were already very close, because of my initial request for patrol officers to move into the area.

As I started to run north on the street, a marked police cruiser turned northbound behind me and was accelerating quickly toward me with the headlights shining on me. I thought to myself, certainly he sees me, as the cruiser was getting closer quickly. I moved toward the west curb trying to get out of the cruiser's path and the cruiser actually angled right with me as I could see the headlights following my path and shining right on me. The cruiser then turned quickly onto the corner parking lot and stopped abruptly.

I turned away from the front of the cruiser as I was just reaching the alley and could not see anyone. As I was stopping, I was thinking to myself, where is Detective L and where are the rest of the detectives moving in for the takedown? Immediately, shots start to ring out to the west and I observe the outline of a dark figure come into view moving slowly from the north side of the alley. There was street lighting in the alley, but I could not make out who the shooter was or what they were shooting at. I thought at the time that it was one of my partners shooting as he was backing on foot, because I knew the suspects would have been running from the northwest and the figure was moving slowly. About twelve to fifteen shots rang out in a matter of three seconds, so I knew it was more than one gun.

At that moment, I saw movement to the north of my position, and I observed one of the black male suspects come running around the corner of a building onto a parking lot directly north of me. I am assuming that several detectives had fired upon a suspect in the alley. I thought they are going to have to take care of the alley and I will take down the suspect north of me.

I turned and ran north toward the suspect and yelled "Police, get on the ground!" The suspect stopped in his path, turned, and ran back westbound on the sidewalk. As the suspect was turning in his stance he dropped the money bag from the robbery. I observed two other cruisers arriving at the intersection to the northeast of that parking lot and I ran through the shine of their headlights toward the fleeing suspect. I continued after the suspect on foot and yelled commands for the suspect to get on the ground. I could see further ahead to the west, Detective N's truck was coming eastbound toward the suspect as the suspect continued running. Detective N turned his truck onto the sidewalk cutting off the suspect's path, so the suspect turned southbound and then, suddenly, gave up.

The suspect threw his hands up into the air and quickly lay on the parking lot. Detective P jumped from the passenger seat of Detective N's truck. I took control of the suspect's arms and Detective P quickly handcuffed him.

I looked directly south from that position and I observed the other two black male suspects run southwest toward the businesses on the south side of the alley and then run in between two businesses southbound. I was very confused how both suspects could have been running, after I had heard all of that gunfire. I started running southbound toward where I observed them both between the businesses. Just before I am crossing the alley, both of them appear back into the light of the alley and run westbound along the rear of those businesses. I called out their direction of travel over the police radio, as I observed Detective F running from behind me and passing me.

The two suspects turned southbound when they reached the end of the building and one was caught right there in the parking lot by Detectives R and F, so I continued running past them toward the third suspect. The last suspect continued running southbound toward the avenue. I observed uniformed K-9 Officer C release his K-9 from the west. I observed the K-9 run up to the suspect and take him to the ground along the south curb of the avenue. There were two uniformed patrol officers right there on the avenue that assisted K-9 Officer C in handcuffing that suspect.

At that moment, I hear Sergeant M and Detective N covering each other on the radio attempting to confirm that all three suspects were in custody. I had observed all three suspects taken into custody and wanted to confirm that all of us detectives were alright. I yelled over the radio, "All three suspects are 10-15 (arrested), is everyone alright?" Within seconds, I hear, "Officer down."

I ran back to the alley, where all of the shots had been fired, and found my partner, Detective L. Detective L was laying on his back along the south side of the alley with his head on uniformed, Officer C's leg.

Detective L cried out to me, "They shot me, Biz, they shot me."

Right away there are questions rushing into my head, what in the hell has happened, how could our takedown have gone so wrong, and how were the suspects able to run so far? I know that shit happens fast, but the good guys are not supposed to lose. Many other detectives and uniformed officers were arriving in the alley. I walked a few feet away from Detective L, so he would not see my concern as I called the dispatcher to the patrol channel. I confirmed with the dispatcher that rescue units knew the exact location where Detective L laid in the alley.

About a minute later, a rescue unit pulled into the alley from the east. I spoke with the rescue personnel as they stepped from their truck to ensure that they knew that the individual shot was an undercover police detective. Next, I spoke to the patrol dispatcher over the radio again and asked if he could coordinate posting a patrol officer at every intersection from our location to the trauma hospital and the dispatcher acknowledged affirmatively. I observed the rescue personnel briefly provide treatment to Detective L, quickly load him, and then start to transport him. I notified Sergeant M that I was going to be in route to notify and pick up Detective L's wife. Sergeant M instructed me to take Detective F with me.

I had been to Detective L's house once before, but was not exactly certain where his residence was located. As I raced toward his neighborhood, initially I was going to get his home address from a dispatcher. Then, I observed Detective L's GPS unit attached to my windshield, so I punched in the "home" button to go to Detective L's residence. My plan was to arrive at the residence and then make a phone call from the front porch to let Detective L's wife know that I was there and something was wrong. As I was arriving, I learned that someone else had merely called Detective L's wife on the phone and she knew we were coming.

Upon arrival, I met with Detective L's wife and she appeared in a calm, state of shock. She advised that her parents were in route to watch their five children that were all sleeping in their residence. I turned and told Detective F that he needed to stay at the residence and watch the sleeping children until her parents arrived. I really did not know the exact status of Detective L, but wanted to get his wife to the hospital and find out. Looking back, I can now laugh at the shocked look that I received from Detective F in regard to my plan.

In my career as a police officer, I had obviously been in several pursuits, and in my capacity as an undercover detective, my driving skills had been put to the test many times. I had no problems with driving Detective L's wife from her house to the trauma hospital as fast as humanly possible. At the time, I thought the best thing that I could do, would be to get her to the hospital quickly, so they could see each other. My plan did pay off, because she was able to see and speak to Detective L, seconds before they took him into surgery. However, Mrs. L would later tell me that she thought that Detective L may not make it, because I was driving so fast and running every red light.

Detective L's brother came into town, while he was still recuperating in the hospital after surgery. Brother A was also in law enforcement and wanted me to take him to show him the scene of the shooting. Sergeant M and I took Brother A out to the scene and walked him through what occurred. It was tough being back at that location, which looked totally different in the daylight. I found a microphone wire that went to Detective L's portable radio. The wire had been cut off of Detective L by rescue units. I, initially, was going to throw it away, as I did not need any reminders of what had occurred.

Just like when Detective P was shot, the events had been playing on and off in my mind. Brother A told me not to leave it anywhere in the alley, so I stuck it into my pocket. Later, I wrapped it into a small bundle and gave it to Brother A as a memento of when Detective L escaped death. I think he appreciated that.

We determined how everything played out that evening. Only two of the three suspects went to do the actual robbery and the third stayed in the alley as the lookout watching the get-away bicycles. Detective L had moved from his east position to the alley, prior to anyone else moving into the alley. Detective L was alone in the alley physically arresting the lookout suspect, when one of the returning robbery suspects started shooting at him. Detective L returned fire and both he and the shooting suspect emptied their guns within three seconds.

I remember telling Detective L the day after surgery, "I know that you must have felt alone in that alley, Detective L, but let me assure you that we were all there around you." Detective L was alone in the alley for about sixty seconds. The physical take-down of all three suspects only took that long, but I am sure that was the longest sixty seconds of Detective L's life. For a long time, and maybe still today, I feel guilty about misreading the shooting scene. From about 125 feet away, I observed the dark figure that appeared along the north side of the alley and that was the shooting suspect. I assumed most detectives were in the alley and I would have been taking down Suspect W by myself. I made the wrong call by not going into the alley and assuming that we had a take-down team of detectives in place. I know that I couldn't have stopped any of the rounds that were fired, but I certainly could have taken away some of those sixty seconds of loneliness.

The surgery was a success for Detective L, but he had a long road to fully recover. Detective L did not have to stay in the hospital for too long after surgery, and was able to recover within six months at home. Detective L returned to our undercover unit, but made an agreement with his wife that he would work dayshift.

The shooter was Suspect S and he was 18 years old and eventually pled to the charges and received 25 years in prison. The other robbery suspect that had gone into the store was Suspect W and he was 17 years old and sentenced to six years in prison as a youthful offender. The lookout robbery suspect was Suspect C and he was 16 years old. The State Attorney's Office only wanted to charge him with escape, so he pled and was sentenced to four years.

Chapter 23

The department decided that it wanted to allocate more assets and manpower to our unit, because both Detectives P and L had been shot within nine months of each other. The staff decided that they would create a dayshift squad and an evening shift squad. Prior to this change, the original SIU detectives were required to always be available to being called in at any time of day and our work schedule always changed based on the time of crime patterns. This new change actually helped us and each squad's work schedule didn't change as frequently. If there was a pattern that required more manpower, then both squads would simply work together. The administration also decided that they wanted to rename the unit, so we obtained a new acronym, C.A.S.E. meaning Crime Awareness Surveillance Enforcement. Not everyone liked the new name.

The senior detectives were basically divided amongst the two shifts, so we had senior detectives on each squad. I stayed on the evening shift, because that is what I always preferred. There were eight new detectives and one new sergeant, so that meant plenty of training.

***

Daytime residential burglary patterns became much more prevalent and many times the evening squad was pulled to work dayshift, because the patterns would become so large. Flat screen televisions had become much more portable and were a common target available in any residence.

We were provided information from the Burglary Unit about a group of juveniles and adults believed to be committing burglaries, so we started surveillance on them. On the first day of surveillance, four of the suspects climbed into a dark green Ford Taurus and went out to do their crimes. The group drove around the City for some time and then eventually went to a heavily residential area and looked for a target. We watched as the group went to a two story home, knocked on the front door, and then knocked down the back door committing their burglary.

We moved in to affect an arrest on the four suspects. I was driving and my new partner at the time was Detective J. Other detectives advised that the suspects were running back to their vehicle and were starting to flee. I was starting to pull into an alley from the west, when Detective S advised that the suspect vehicle with two suspects was fleeing westbound. I observed the suspect vehicle coming out of a bend in the alley and started accelerating toward my undercover vehicle. I stopped about twenty feet into the mouth of the alley and observed the suspect accelerate his vehicle as fast as it would go. There was nowhere for the suspect to pass me and I guess he thought that he could simply drive through my vehicle. The suspect rammed into the front of my vehicle at approximately 35 miles per hour and with tremendous force. The airbags in both vehicles went off and I was thrown forward into the airbag and steering wheel.

The airbag dust and steam from the radiators that had exploded was just starting to settle, when I observed the suspects start to jump from their vehicle and try to flee on foot. We were able to catch the one passenger at the crash scene and the driver was caught just a short distance away. All of the suspects were charged with the burglary and the driver was charged with aggravated battery against law enforcement officers. A judge sentenced the driver to nine months, time served, for all of his offenses, including ramming us in our police vehicle. The driver was released from jail and within six months killed an innocent motorist in a hit and run fatality.

**

My undercover vehicle was out of commission for almost a month since they had to put an entire new front end on it after being rammed. I simply told my wife that my truck was in the shop getting some extra work done on it. It was not too unusual for me to drive different undercover vehicles and I almost never told my wife about trips to the emergency room.

About two months after getting my truck back, we were working an evening shift. Officer L was my new partner and I was driving. We were simply driving around looking for crime, when we started watching a white male that was walking in a residential neighborhood. The subject was continuing to walk westbound and I had stopped my vehicle on a two lane street facing north along the east curb. Basically, we were parked and watching the subject from a stationary position with the lights on our vehicle off.

A couple of minutes later, I observed a car in my driver's side mirror as it made a northbound turn onto our same street from a busy avenue two blocks south of our position. My attention was switching back and forth from the subject walking and the approaching vehicle. I did realize that the vehicle had accelerated to a speed of about 45 miles per hour, so I started to focus more on the vehicle. It came to a point, where I fully expected to observe the approaching vehicle to naturally drive around my vehicle. The vehicle came closer and I could only see the driver's side headlight. I expected to quickly see both of the vehicle's headlights, but the vehicle actually drove even closer to the curb and I realized that the vehicle was going to hit the rear of our vehicle.

I did not have any time to warn Detective L. I simply stated, "Oh, no!" and braced for the impact. The vehicle crashed directly into the rear of our parked vehicle at approximately 45 miles per hour and the impact was terrible. We were both thrown backward into the seat

211

and then bounced forward. My vehicle was knocked about twenty-five feet north from where we were parked.

I notified other members of our unit about the crash over our police radio channel and asked for them to have patrol units respond. I exited my vehicle to check on the status of anyone in the other vehicle. As I approached, I observed a white female driver still in the driver's seat pushing on the accelerator. I shut the female's vehicle off and asked her if she needed rescue. The female tried to get out of the driver's side door, but it was partially crushed in the closed position from the impact. Next, the female jumped over to the passenger side door and attempted to get out. Detective P made it on scene at this moment and stated, "Where is the driver?" as he looked into her vehicle. I responded with an aggravated, "Yeah"!? Then Detective P helped me get the intoxicated female driver out of her vehicle.

Once out of the vehicle, the female driver looked at the two vehicles crashed together and I guess made her own intoxicated analysis of the situation. The female stated, "Alright, no police, no police, I will so take care of you" as she implied sexual favors. With a blank look, I stated, "Ma'am I am the police". The intoxicated female's face dropped in disappointment as she stated, "You are the police." The female was later arrested for DUI by patrol officers that responded to the scene.

Once again my vehicle was back in the shop for repairs, and this time I would get an entire rear end for the truck. Detective L and I went for a complimentary trip to the emergency room and were given the usual, 800 milligram Ibuprofen.

***

There were also residential burglary patterns that occurred at night. We referred to them as creep-in burglaries, because the suspect would have to assume that someone was home sleeping. These patterns

212

always took a high priority, due to the potential for them to turn into sexual assaults.

We started working a pattern of a creep-in burglary in a somewhat secluded neighborhood in the City. I was sitting in my vehicle by myself at about 0200 hours and out of nowhere, someone bangs on my front passenger window. I drew my handgun, but kept it out of sight. I lowered the front passenger window barely and stated, "What the fuck do you want?" There was a 40 year old black male at the window, who would later become our burglary suspect. The suspect started to tell me how he was lost and then he walked quickly around to my driver's side window, so I lowered that window slightly. The suspect then asked me if I knew where Bay Street was located. Now, Bay Street was located about one hundred yards east of my vehicle, but I needed to convince the suspect that I wasn't the police or any threat to him.

I stated in an aggravated tone, "I have no fucking idea." I continued to tell the suspect that I lived in another city and I was "down here looking for my wife". I started to ask the suspect if he knew of or had seen my wife and he quickly became disinterested. I watched as the suspect walked eastbound away from my vehicle and into the area where the creep-in burglaries were occurring. I informed other detectives that we needed to start surveillance of this suspect.

Eventually, I observed the suspect continue into an alley a couple blocks to the east. All of our units were working to maintain the surveillance, but we lost the suspect's location somewhere in that alley. A few minutes later, Sergeant M asked for someone to check along the front of the residences to the south. As soon as I started walking westbound on that avenue, the same black male suspect jumped over a privacy fence and started walking toward me.

A surveillance detective does not want to be seen at all, much less twice. I had grabbed a dog leash from my truck before I started walking on foot. As the suspect approached, I asked him if he had seen a black Lab running around. The suspect advised that he had not and continued walking past me. When the suspect was just steps away, I stated "My dog is real friendly and if you find her, I'll give you twenty bucks." The suspect acknowledged and walked away eastbound. I knew that the suspect really didn't see me in the darkness of my truck earlier, but was surprised that he didn't recognize my voice. I advised other units over the radio of the suspect's position and the fact that I spoke to him again.

The suspect continued looking for a target house and continued in and out of alleys and continued to walk eastbound. At this point, I simply tried to stay out of the surveillance as I couldn't be seen again. The suspect finally located a house that he liked. The suspect climbed up an exterior stairwell to a second floor door and walked right inside. I would have to guess that the suspect had been there before. After a few minutes, the suspect came walking out slowly and then started running. During this burglary the suspect woke the homeowner.

The suspect ran downstairs and attempted to run northbound in the alley, but we took him to the ground and handcuffed him. The homeowner victim started after the suspect with a handgun. Detectives had to quickly advise the victim that we were the police, and instructed him to secure his weapon back inside his residence. We ended the creep-in burglary pattern and the suspect didn't even recognize me as I assisted in handcuffing him.

***

One evening shift, Detective W and I were simply driving around looking for crime. We were aware of an auto theft suspect that was wanted and the location of his residence. We had never seen the suspect outside and there was an old vehicle in the front yard that never moved. However, on this night we finally observed the old vehicle on the road as it drove up to a Checkers drive through restaurant.

The suspect only lived about two blocks from the Checkers restaurant, so we had to do something quick to place him under arrest. We had called other detectives in our unit, but no other detectives were close enough. I dropped Detective W off on foot and then moved toward the parking lot of the Checkers restaurant. I was in position to box the suspect vehicle when he came through the drive through, but needed some help from other detectives.

The suspect had completed his order and was starting to leave, but no other units were on scene. Detective W and I decided to take the opportunity and took the suspect down by ourselves.

At that time, I was driving a terrible surveillance vehicle, which was a small two door Hyundai Genesis. I pulled the little car toward the front of the suspect's vehicle as he was pulling out of the drive through and I think my driving simply confused him so he stopped. Detective W had run right up to the suspect's driver's door on foot and had his gun pointed at the suspect. The suspect was arrested by the two of us and our little Hyundai.

***

I always enjoyed hunting down wanted subjects. Some would be wanted for crimes that they recently committed and others were for old warrants. The areas of responsibilities in our unit were divided among detectives, so we wouldn't duplicate efforts and I always chose fugitives. At one time, there were two detectives assigned to fugitives, so I facetiously called the two of us the Fugitive Unit. Detective C was assigned to dayshift

and I was evenings. I told Detective C he could be called
FU and I would be FU2.

***

I was working an evening shift with my assigned
partner Detective W. We were not working a specific
pattern, so I was thumbing through my list of fugitives.
We decided to check on a 45 year old white male that
had a known residence and active warrants for
narcotics. We drove past the residence and could see
lights on inside and four vehicles out on the front yard.
We decided to sit and watch the residence for a little
while.

After about thirty minutes, we observed a white male
approach the front door of the residence. The white
male spoke with someone at the door and left within a
minute. We decided to stop the white male and
question him as he was leaving. The white male had
just made it back to the street, when I asked him, "Hey,
is Suspect T home". The white male took one look at
Detective W and I and started backing away. The white
male advised that the suspect was inside the residence
and quickly walked away from the scene.

Detective W and I knocked on the door and the
wanted suspect opened the door. We both stepped into
the residence and took custody of Suspect T's arms.
The suspect began resisting and pulling away from us.
We had identified ourselves as police officers, but had to
continue fighting with the suspect until he was into
handcuffs. The overweight suspect was just sitting
there in his boxer shorts, so we asked his wife to get
him some clothes and shoes. The wife helped him get
into clothing, as the suspect explained that he was
unemployed and addicted to prescription pain
medication for a back injury. Suspect T continued
talking and told us that we were lucky that he didn't
really fight us.

We called for a uniformed officer to respond to transport the suspect to jail. We stood the suspect up and he kissed his crying wife goodbye on the front porch. We walked the suspect out to the marked cruiser. The suspect turned back to look at his wife, who was still crying on the front porch. The suspect stated, "Don't cry honey, what are you crying about?" As I looked over the top of four broken down vehicles toward the house that was in desperate need of repair, I could see the wife crying as she watched her drug addicted, unemployed husband being taken to jail. The suspect turned to both Detective W and I and stated, "You all may think I have nothing, but two of those cars in the yard are Lexus." I have probably never observed a man more detached from reality than him.

Unfortunately, as soon as we walked away, I realized that my left elbow was injured during the struggle. I ended up getting referred to an orthopedic surgeon, who wanted to do surgery for a partially torn bicep tendon. Prior to that injury, I was in great shape and had been working out at least four days per week. I was strong and healthy, and I could bench press 300 pounds. I didn't know at the time, but that would be last time in my life that I could make that statement.

Chapter 24

Our unit started working another armed robbery pattern to convenience stores and small businesses like a beauty supply store. There had already been four robberies prior to us working the robbery pattern. The area in the City where the robberies were occurring was very spread out and we did not have the ability to cover every potential business. We did have information from prior reports and surveillance video that told us there were two black males and they were armed with semi-automatic handguns.

The very first day that we worked the pattern, a robbery was dispatched to a convenience store that no detectives were near and the suspects were able to get away. The video from that robbery provided us with a good image of one of the suspects wearing a light gray hoodie, sweatshirt with an image of a monkey on the front. That sweatshirt was confirmed to have been also used in another one of the robberies in the pattern.

On the sixth day working the robbery pattern, a robbery occurred prior to our check-on time and later that same day another robbery occurred at a convenience store where no detectives were close. Once again, the suspects were able to get away. It was very unusual for our unit to start working a pattern and not catch the suspects on their very next offense. The gray sweatshirt was once again worn in both of the robberies on that date.

Detective C had done some great research and developed a potential suspect named Suspect C. We were working very closely with the robbery detectives and the robbery sergeant at the time did not believe that Suspect C was involved. Based on Detective C's information, we started surveillance of Suspect C and followed him all over the City.

On the eighth day of working the pattern, we observed Suspect C get into a green Subaru Outback that was driven by a black female and also had an unknown black male passenger. The black female drove to the alley behind a convenience store and dropped off the two black males. Both Detective F and I were able to confirm that one of the black males was wearing a light gray hoodie sweatshirt with the same monkey image on the front. The two black males also had gloves and had their faces partially covered.

The two remained in the alley behind the store for approximately two minutes and then decided to leave on foot in a northeast direction, which was the direction that the suspect vehicle left. The two black male suspects climbed back into the Subaru and the female drove them back to the known residence. They only stayed for approximately seven minutes and then left again.

They drove straight to a large shopping plaza, which included a grocery store, a Dollar General, and several smaller businesses. The female drove the Subaru around the shopping plaza and circulated a little to the west. I took a position on foot inside the shopping plaza, but we still did not know which business they were possibly targeting. Detectives advised over the radio that the two black male suspects exited the Subaru southwest of the complex and were approaching on foot. I decided to move to the inside of a small Italian restaurant for a minute until I knew which business they were headed toward. The minute I stepped into the restaurant, I had a very attentive waitress trying to help me. The waitress asked if I would like to sit and then if I wanted to see a menu. I observed a stack of small paper placemats full of advertisements and picked one up. I told the waitress that I just wanted to stand there and look at "this" for a minute, which I am sure confused her.

During that time the suspects were getting closer and eventually made their way to the Dollar General store. I watched as both hooded black males entered the store with their faces covered and hoods on their heads. I could see a portion of the registers at the front from my position and Detective P confirmed that the robbery was in-progress. I identified myself as a police officer to the waitress and about five patrons of the restaurant and confirmed that they understood that I was a police officer, because I wanted to pull out my firearm. I pulled out a police badge that hung from a chain around my neck and stood just inside the doorway of the restaurant with my issued Glock semi-automatic handgun in my right hand.

I observed Suspect B come running out of the Dollar General first and head back westbound. Right behind him was Suspect C, who was carrying a black semi-automatic handgun and fumbling with what I assumed was a money bag up against his chest. The two continued at a jog westbound, as I came out of the Italian restaurant north of them and ran in their direction.

I ran southbound and then westbound through the same path that the suspects had taken. I observed and heard other detectives start to challenge the two suspects as they were now running southbound along the west side of the Dollar General store. Both suspects quickly turned around and ran back northbound toward my position. Suspect B was tall and skinny and ran faster than Suspect C and I observed Suspect B run past Suspect C along that west wall. There were probably thirty officers and detectives on scene and many officers were challenging both suspects to stop and get on the ground.

To my east, I observed Detectives P and T running toward the front of the Dollar General Store entrance to secure the business. I was not going to let either of the suspects make it to a point where they could turn back eastbound toward that entrance or toward any of the businesses in the plaza. I was the only officer between the suspects and the front entrance to the business they had just robbed. I had previously yelled, "Police, get on the ground" and I was still planting my feet and just about to shoot Suspect B, who was in front running. I remembered that Suspect C was the one that was carrying the firearm and could possibly be a bigger threat to me. I glanced toward Suspect C and could see him running with the firearm still in his hand and it was tilted at an angle, but pointed right at me. Suspect C was just turning his head around from looking at officers challenging him from behind and he looked right at me. I yelled, "Police" fired two rounds and then yelled, "Drop the gun".

After the second shot, Suspect C's firearm was flying up into the air about a foot over his head. The gun had the same forward momentum that Suspect C also had. I immediately took a couple steps to the east cutting off Suspect B's path and yelled, "Get on the ground." Suspect B threw his hands into the air as high as he could get them, threw himself up against the concrete wall, and he turned to watch Suspect C falling toward the concrete after being shot.

The firearm flew out of Suspect C's hand on the south side of a parked car, bounced under that car, and rested just under the edge of the north side of that parked car. Suspect C's momentum carried him to the north side of that parked car also and he went to the ground with the firearm barely out of reach.

At the same time, Detectives P and T heard the shots from the entrance of the Dollar General Store and came running around the corner to secure Suspect B into handcuffs. Detective G had run up from the west as Suspect C landed on his stomach and stretched his hands forward. As he extended his hands forward, he was reaching within inches of the firearm and I thought

I was going to have to shoot him again. Detective G handcuffed Suspect C without any further resistance.

A couple years later, Suspect B pled and was sentenced to fifteen years in prison and Suspect C pled and was sentenced to twenty years in prison.

***

During one of the days that we were working the above armed robbery pattern, a call of a man with a gun was dispatched over the radio. The caller provided a detailed description of a 17 year old black male and the clothing that he was wearing. The caller advised that the suspect was showing the gun off to his friends at the city park and the caller then advised that the black male was starting to leave the park.

A few of the detectives in my unit were not too far away from the location of the park, so Sergeant H advised for us to respond. I arrived first and located a black male matching the clothing description walking out of the park westbound with a young black female. The two subjects entered an alley that continued in a westbound direction from the street.

I exited my vehicle and advised for Detective F to get a little to the west, as he came into the area. As I was watching the two subjects walk westbound, I observed the black male take out a black semi-automatic handgun and hold it in his right hand as he continued walking away from me. I advised other units that the suspect did in fact have a firearm and that he was holding it in his right hand. I advised for uniformed units to start to move up and I was going to challenge the suspect in the alley.

I approached behind the suspect and when I was approximately twenty-five feet behind him, I yelled, "Police, drop the gun!" The suspect and the female with him were startled by my command. The suspect turned in a clockwise direction toward me. The firearm was still in his right hand as it crossed between us, but he

223

never raised it up toward me. I could see the startled look on the suspects face, as he observed me standing with my firearm pointed right at him. As the suspect was completing his turn, he released his hold on the handgun and it fell to the ground to the right of the suspect as he faced me.

I yelled for the suspect to get on the ground and he complied as Detective F came up from the west and quickly handcuffed the suspect. The firearm was determined to have been stolen in a residential burglary just one week prior. I charged the 17 year old suspect with carrying a concealed firearm and grand theft and then burglary detectives interviewed him. The suspect was transported to the juvenile jail.

***

I was placed on administrative leave with full pay due to the shooting of Suspect C and that shooting investigation. About two months prior to this shooting, I had the injury to my left elbow and was simply trying to put off having the surgery. Since I knew I would be off for a couple weeks, I quickly scheduled the elbow surgery, where they repaired the torn bicep tendon.

Up to that point in my life, I had already had five previous orthopedic surgeries for injuries to various parts of my body. I was familiar with recovering from surgery and how to progress with rehabilitation. In hindsight, the recovery from that surgery was a little different and probably the first time that I should have known something was not right with my health. I was having trouble with rehabilitation and could not physically twist my elbow anymore. I assumed that it was a complication from the surgery itself.

Technically, I never took any time off of work for the surgery and rehabilitation, because I simply returned to work as soon as I was cleared in the shooting by the State Attorney's Office and our Internal Affairs Division, which ended my administrative leave.

Chapter 25

I had only been back to work for two weeks, when I received the worst call of my career early one morning. I was off-duty and at home, when Officer J called to let me know that Sergeant B had just been shot. At the time, Officer J did not know the status of Sergeant B. I had worked very closely for years with Sergeant B as a CPO and he and I made the "Rush Limbaugh" arrest together. I raced to the shooting scene in my undercover vehicle and threw on all of my equipment along the way. Upon arrival at the location, I realized that I was all too familiar with the specific address. The shooter was Suspect L, an individual that I had been trying to locate and arrest a few months earlier for outstanding warrants. I had been pulled away with working the armed robbery pattern that had ended with my shooting and the elbow surgery.

There was already a crowd of about one hundred law enforcement officers and almost as many citizens standing at the intersection to the west of Suspect L's residence. Suspect L was barricaded inside the attic of his residence and the SWAT Team was still trying to get him out. There were a few reporters setting up on scene with cameras, so I approached with a hooded sweatshirt and no visible identification. I was stopped by a couple of deputies from the county and had to identify myself. Our dayshift was working that day, but I was still assigned to the evening shift.

Eventually, I made contact with Detective C on the radio and he wanted me to give him a call. Detective C asked me to respond to the trauma hospital and meet with K-9 Officer Y's wife. I asked Detective C how K-9 Officer Y was involved and what was his status? This was the first that I had heard that any other officer was even involved, and I learned at that moment that K-9 Officer Y was killed.

K-9 Officer Y and I had about the same time on the police department, as he joined the force two classes after mine. We had worked the same district for years in patrol, had married about the same time in our lives, had taken our honeymoons in Hawaii, and had even purchased the exact same model home in the same neighborhood by coincidence. My friend K-9 Officer Y was killed and I was going to the hospital to meet with his wife.

I arrived at the hospital to find it as busy as I have ever seen it to be. I parked my undercover vehicle over a curb and onto a grassy area near the emergency room. Everywhere I looked there were traumatized police officers. As I walked into the emergency room, I learned that Sergeant B had also died from the gunshot wounds. Sergeant B had rushed inside the suspect's residence to save K-9 Officer Y, after the initial shots were fired at the scene. I entered the emergency room and found the room, where they had just taken K-9 Officer Y. The hospital staff was just finishing cleaning him up to make him presentable for family. I located K-9 Officer Y's wife just outside those doors. I hugged Mrs. Y and followed her back into the room to see K-9 Officer Y. Nothing seemed to be real and I am sure we were both in a state of shock. Mrs. Y showed me the additional injuries to K-9 Officer Y.

K-9 Officer Y had been shot in the head and most certainly died instantly. The hospital staff had wrapped his entire head with the exception of his face. I stayed with Mrs. Y for a few minutes and learned that K-9 Officer Y's father was almost to the hospital and had not heard of the death, yet. I went into a back room of the emergency room with a group of K-9 officers, where Mr. Y was going to be informed of the death of his son. It just does not seem normal for a parent to have to learn of the death of a child, but a parent should never have to hear that their child was murdered. Mr. Y arrived and was quickly pulled into that back room to learn about the death of his son. I recognized Mr. Y from seeing him playing with his grandchildren at the neighborhood park and talking with him there. There are not words to properly describe the reactions of Mr. Y.

I left that room thirty minutes later and observed the Chief of Police H talking with a group of about thirty police officers within the emergency area of the hospital. Chief H was discussing the release of information and the names of the deceased to the media and the fact that he did not have any control over the release. I encouraged Chief H to organize a timely release of that information later in the day, so close family and friends could be notified.

Eventually, K-9 Officer Y's mother and a sister that lived locally made it to the hospital and were informed. After an hour, a decision was made to take the family back to K-9 Officer Y's residence. The family's mini-van was brought up to the emergency room doors for them to load up into, but no one had planned to drive them home. I gave the keys to my undercover vehicle to another officer at the emergency room exit and climbed into the mini-van to take K-9 Officer Y's family to his home.

The family was obviously still in a state of shock and still had not been able to provide the death notification to another sister that lived in Georgia. The family had numerous questions for me along the way and many of them I could not answer. I stayed at the residence for some time, but eventually needed some time to myself. The funeral for both officers was just a few days later and we buried two of my friends.

I had held the assignment of monitoring fugitives or wanted subjects within our unit for years. I always kept an active log of about twenty various wanted subjects throughout the entire City that I considered a priority.

Suspect L, the shooter, was on my list and I had made several trips to two different known residences looking for him. Due to the robbery pattern and my shooting, it had been three months since I had looked for Suspect L.

Detective W and I had actually held surveillance on the residence where the shooting had occurred three months earlier. On one of the evenings, there was some activity at the residence as we watched from the west. We saw some movement near the front of the residence and we called for another detective to try to get a look at anyone that was possibly out in front of the residence. Suspect L also had a brother that was similar to his size. We continued to try to watch the front of the residence as we held to the west. One of our Detectives was able to get a partial view to confirm someone in the front yard, but was not able to obtain the identification due to it being dark. We observed a vehicle leave the residence, but our detectives were still getting into position and we never had a chance to stop that vehicle or verify the identity of the driver. No one can change the past, but I wish that I had focused on arresting Suspect L more intently and obviously the shootings would not have occurred.

***

One month later, it was evening shift's day off and I was home about to go to bed. I received a call from Detective T and received even more tragic news. Detective T advised that he had just received information that Patrol Officer C had been shot four times in the chest. Detective T did not know the status of Officer C, but was headed into work.

Once again, I found myself rushing in to another chaotic scene. Detective T did not have to tell me the status of Officer C, because I think I knew. Officer C was a tough old school cop that had just over 25 years on the street. Officer C had always been in patrol and the majority of that time was spent on the midnight shift. Officer C was a great cop with natural police instincts, but never wore a ballistic vest. I had worked many off-duty jobs with Officer C and also worked closely with him on several midnight crime patterns.

I made it into work and learned that Officer C had been shot and killed. The suspect was still at large and officers had already set up a perimeter around an extremely large area. My unit and the undercover Vice and Narcotics Unit was teamed together and tasked with clearing an entire city park and looking for any potential evidence. The search started sometime close to midnight and did not end until close to 0800 hours. During the search of the park, I recovered a dark blue sweatshirt that I had to testify about later in court.

After our search of the park, both units simply continued looking for the suspect through the neighborhood to the south of the park. The next eleven blocks to the south were primarily residential and encompassed my old CPO area as well as some of CPO Officer B's zone. Since I knew both areas better than anyone, I worked with the Vice and Narcotic Lieutenant to keep the search organized. After approximately eight hours of searching, our team was sent home. We were all exhausted, but no one wanted to leave. That next day, the parents of the shooter, Suspect L, turned him into detectives.

Deceased Officer C and Patrol Officer Z had simply been dispatched to a suspicious individual call. Officer C had probably handled over a thousand similar suspicious calls over the course of his 25 year career. Officer C observed Suspect L and checked out with him to obtain his information and ensure that he was not involved in any criminal activity. Without warning, Suspect L shot Officer C four times in the chest. Suspect L later stated that he was simply "afraid" of Officer C and started shooting.

Suspect L had just turned 16 years of age. Of course some of the media, played to the tune of these actions being those of an impulsive teenager. An impulsive teenager may steal a shirt from Dillard's or drink beer before turning legal age, but an impulsive teenager does not fire four rounds into the chest of another human being, much less do anything to harm a police officer. This shooting was the act of pure evil. The defense also tried to utilize the defendant's age to his advantage and actually filed legal motions claiming that Suspect L had never had any encounter with the police, like that was some kind of legal justification for shooting Officer C.

About eight months prior to that shooting, our unit had arrested Suspect L and two other suspects, after their stolen Ford F-150 ran out of gas. We initially conducted surveillance on the stolen vehicle and then watched as it stopped and the three suspects tried to push it off the roadway. We all moved in to affect the arrest and all three suspects fled on foot and were caught. I had caught and handcuffed Suspect L on that auto theft offense, so I was subpoenaed for deposition and for the legal motion in the homicide trial to disprove the claims of the defense. Eventually, Suspect L was convicted and sentenced to life in prison, but that does little to ease the pain of losing another friend and a fellow police officer.

Approximately eleven years prior to the shooting of Officer C, I had arrested Suspect L's father, who was Suspect L, sr. I was on patrol one day in full uniform and I was advised by Sergeant D that he located a 1985 Oldsmobile Cutlass Supreme bearing an improper tag. I initiated a traffic stop on the vehicle in an attempt to stop it for Sergeant D. The suspect, driver, refused to stop for my cruiser, so I advised this information over the radio. I had turned away from the vehicle, as required by our pursuit regulations, and had gone partially around the block. I observed the vehicle pulled up into a yard approximately four blocks from my original traffic stop and I could see the driver walking toward the front door of the residence. I called for back-up units to respond, drove to the residence, and pulled up into the front yard. I jumped out of my cruiser and yelled to the suspect as he was standing on the front porch with a female later determined to be his sister.

As I ran toward Suspect L, sr., I yelled for him to not enter the residence. The suspect looked right at me and ran inside. The sister went in behind him and slammed the door, as I reached the front porch. I hit the front door splintering the doorframe and causing the door to fly open. I caught a glimpse of the suspect as he ran left down a hallway. I pulled my issued firearm and notified units over the radio that I was inside the residence. There were three to four other unidentified subjects inside the residence. I entered the hallway and yelled for the suspect to come out. The suspect came out of one of the back bedrooms. I took control of the suspect, exited the residence, and handcuffed him outside as other units arrived.

The arrests in the past of Suspect L or any of his family didn't really matter, because that story still ended with the death of my friend, Officer C.

Chapter 26

About a month after Officer C was killed. I was still working my regular evening shift and still going to physical therapy for my left elbow. The surgery was deemed a success, but I did not seem to be healing as I normally would. I was slowly regaining the ability to twist the elbow, but started having a very visible new tremor in my left hand. I noticed that the tremor seemed to be accentuated by any pain, especially when I had pain in the elbow at physical therapy. I continued going to the orthopedic surgeon and to physical therapy, but decided to also find a neurologist on my own.

The neurologist was Dr. B and she specialized in movement disorders. Dr. B advised that she believed I possibly had a tremor that was common and known as Essential Tremor. I was prescribed some medication that was supposed to minimize the tremor, but don't believe it ever had any effect. I also started to become very anxious for no reason and had night sweats on and off. In fact, my sleep habits were terrible and some nights I would only get a couple of hours of sleep. Even my thinking had changed and everything that I did took a great deal of effort. My assumption at the time was that I was having signs and symptoms of PTSD or post-traumatic stress disorder. I certainly had been through a great deal and observed many things as a police officer.

Initially, I simply tried to ignore all of the problems and hoped they would go away. Does that ever work? I continued to have the symptoms and noticed that the anxiety would become worse when I had to go to court. The tremor was initially minimal, but not controllable in my left hand and had also started a little in my voice. I believe it was the environment of the courthouse being so formal that made the symptoms seem worse. I knew there would be no easy way to excuse myself in any court setting, if the uncontrolled symptoms started.

Luckily, I remember only one testimony to a State Attorney, where I completely fell apart and my mind almost would not function. The case was a child abuse offense that included an aggravated battery to another motorist. I witnessed a mother completely lose it and in a fit of road rage rammed another vehicle off of the roadway. The mother had three children in the vehicle and we followed her and arrested her right after committing the offense. The testimony was as simple as that.

There were three detectives involved with the offense, so we all three simply went into the room to testify together. I entered the room feeling great. As soon as we sat down for testimony, I suddenly felt as if I were under physical attack and felt trapped. The three detectives were given two chairs with our back to the entry door of the room and I was squeezed in the middle of the other two detectives. I felt trapped and could not think clearly about the details of the case. The trapped feelings only brought on additional stress and the uncontrollable tremors. The crazy thing that I could not understand was in the past I loved testifying in court. One of my favorite parts of the job was to walk into a deposition or courtroom setting and establish the truth through bantering with defense attorneys.

I developed another unusual change that I really didn't fully recognize until at least a year later. During that time period, I became very emotional or couldn't control my emotions. I would even become lightly teary eyed during sad movie scenes which never happened in the past. I remember telling Dr. B that I felt real emotional, "like a woman" and I am sure she loved hearing that. I don't really know if part of the problems were side effects from the medication. I just kept going to work and hoped that the medication would help the symptoms, but I continued to get worse.

***

One of our detectives located a stolen vehicle. We conducted surveillance until we had an opportunity to arrest the driver. The driver was an 18 year old black male named Suspect B. The story would have ended there, but Suspect B decided to make an ass of himself at the rear of the police station. Suspect B was sitting in the rear of a marked police cruiser parked at the police station. Detectives were completing all of the paperwork and then were going to put him onto the prisoner transport van. Suspect B started yelling something from inside the cruiser to get attention, so I opened the door to see if he needed something.

Suspect B stated, "I am looking at all you undercovers and I am going to know all of your faces." I simply replied, "Well, take a good look at my face, because the next time you see it I will be kicking your fucking ass!" I closed the cruiser door and Suspect B didn't have anything further to say to us.

***

Detective W and I made a pretty good team. Both of us liked to be involved and loved to make arrests. I still had the responsibility of monitoring the wanted subjects or fugitives. When we were not working a specific pattern, a great deal of our time was locating suspects that did not want to be found. There were hundreds of new warrants issued every month by the county court and old warrants needed to be taken off my list after the suspects were arrested by any officer.

One evening, Detective W and I went to the neighborhood of an 18 year old white male that had active warrants for auto theft and battery. The suspect's last known address was with his parents at this location. The residence appeared in disrepair and there were a couple of vehicles in the driveway. We decided to attempt to speak with a few of the neighbors to see if we could confirm whether the suspect had been seen at his residence recently. I had a previous arrest photograph of the suspect with me to show to the neighbors, if they appeared helpful.

We knocked on the door of the house that was on the opposite corner of the intersection from the suspect's residence. An 18 year old white male with no shirt opened the door and he looked strangely familiar. Detective W and I almost looked at each other in disbelief, because our wanted suspect had just answered the neighbor's door. We took custody of the white male and placed him into handcuffs. We called for a uniformed patrol officer to respond to transport the arrested suspect to jail and we were simply standing on the front porch of that residence waiting.

An extremely intoxicated, 50 year old, white male came walking along the sidewalk northbound past the front of the residence. The drunk must have taken issue with us standing at the residence, because he started yelling things to us. Initially, the drunk asked what we were doing and then started cursing at us telling us we needed to leave the neighborhood. We informed the drunk that we were police officers and asked him to continue on his way. The drunk decided to walk to the residence next door and lean against the back of a parked vehicle. For the next seven minutes, Detective W and I ignored the constant banter and cursing from the drunk.

The uniformed patrol officer arrived and took custody of the arrested suspect. We advised the uniformed officer that we would take care of all of the documentation and the responsibility of removing the warrant from the system and thanked him for transporting. Even during this time, the drunk continued rambling and cursing as he leaned against that vehicle.

I could not help myself or miss the opportunity to express to the drunk what I thought of him and his actions. As we walked away from the scene, I stated a loud exaggerated, "Thank you again officer for all of your help" toward the uniformed officer. Within the same breath, I turned and pointed toward the drunk and stated, "And you, Sir, can go fuck yourself!"

***

There were a couple of instances where I had the opportunity to help out fellow officers with non-police related issues, or what some would refer to as keeping fuel in their vehicles. We were working evening shift one night and I received a call from Detective P about midnight. Detective P advised me that he had run out of gas. Detective P did not live too far from the area and he knew that he had a gas can on his rear porch. Detective P asked me to pick up the gas can and deliver it to him on the side of the road.

Another time, we were all working surveillance on an arson suspect. I received a call from Sergeant H to meet him at his location. I pulled up to Sergeant H's vehicle and he climbed out of his vehicle and into mine. Sergeant H instructed me to drive him to our office. About halfway to the office, Sergeant H finally admitted that he had run out of gas and needed to pick up the gas can from our office.

I have never been one to rub someone's nose into their honest mistake, because I always thought that next time it might be my mistake. I believe that both officers asked me to help because they knew that I could keep their secret. Now, everyone knows.

***

Throughout my career, there were numerous retirement parties for officers that had finished their careers. The parties were always held in the basement of the station at 1400 hours and would be attended by an average of 75 fellow police department employees. The group usually included the officer's entire chain of command up to the chief of police. At the start of the party, the room would always be quiet for parting words or any awards coming from the chain of command for the retiring officer. After the presentation, there would be a large sheet cake and drinks with everyone socializing.

At the time, our unit was assigned and still using Nextel phones for whenever we needed to communicate anything that we did not want to go over the police radio. The Nextel phone operated as a cell phone and a two-way radio. Once you had shared the connect code of the phone, your friends could speak to you directly over the two-way radio simply by talking into their phone. We all usually left the external speaker on, so we wouldn't miss anyone else calling.

On this particular day, Sergeant G was retiring and I was arriving about seven minutes late, so the formal presentation had already started. I was walking up to the rear door of the police station, when I remembered to turn off the external speaker on my phone. Detective W had already made it into the retirement party and was inside the basement, so I thought I would "help" him out too. I called Detective W over the Nextel two-way radio and stated in a loud clear voice, "Hey, Detective W, don't forget to turn off your speaker on your phone!" I entered the basement retirement party and observed a number of people around Detective W smiling and laughing and Chief of Police H was still speaking up front.

***

Detective W and I had driven up to an apartment complex that had recently had a few vehicle burglaries committed. As we entered, I observed a security guard on a golf cart driving around. I wanted to stay inside the complex for a little while, so I decided to quietly notify the security guard that we were officers and would be in the complex. After speaking to the security guard we monitored the activity within the apartment complex.

After about an hour, the security guard decided to come and ask us a question. We had been inside the complex undetected for all of this time and now the security guard was potentially announcing our presence by speaking to us in the middle of the complex. The security guard came up to my driver's side window and started to tell us about some juveniles that were playing with a turtle near the retention pond earlier in the week. He advised that he made the juveniles leave the turtle alone. Next, the security guard wanted to know about any State of Florida statutes that dealt with turtles.

I turned away from the security guard and asked, "Hey, Detective W, do you know about turtle law?" Detective W was having a hard time keeping his composure and playing along. I turned back to the security guard and explained to him that the Florida Fish Game and Wildlife agency dealt with turtle law and we were not aware of those statutes. We ended up leaving the complex and assumed that our cover had been blown.

***

One evening shift, we were notified by uniformed patrol officers that they had located a wanted suspect that was getting onto a motorcycle. The patrol officers advised that they were quite certain that he was not going to stop for a marked cruiser, because the suspect had fled from them in the past.

We responded to the area and detectives in our unit were able to locate the motorcycle as it left the area. We conducted surveillance on the motorcycle for a few minutes and the suspect began to drive very reckless and at high speeds. Detective W and I observed the suspect make a reckless U-turn on a four lane road and then accelerate quickly in the opposite direction. We were not certain if the suspect always drove this way on his motorcycle.

There was other vehicle traffic in the area, so we were able to also turn around and continue to follow at a great distance. I was trying to maintain visual contact on the motorcycle and advised other units of the suspect's location, but the motorcycle was about seven blocks ahead of us. Suddenly, I observed the tail light of the motorcycle leave the roadway and appear to drive on the north sidewalk. I saw the tail light continue westbound and then it disappeared.

We drove the seven blocks up to the last point where we had observed the motorcycle. We observed two vehicles stopped along the north side of the roadway and called for uniformed officers to respond to check out with them. We continued driving for another half a block and then observed the motorcycle lying on its' side in a church parking lot. We notified other detectives and started to look for the suspect to the north. We located and arrested the suspect in an alley to the north. After a brief struggle, the suspect was handcuffed.

The suspect tried to swerve around another vehicle on the road, but hit that vehicle with his handlebar. The impact caused a severe laceration to the suspect's finger. The suspect was taken to the hospital and they had to amputate that finger.

***

One night, Detective W and I decided to look for an aggravated battery suspect that had an active warrant. The suspect's last known address was outside the City in the jurisdiction of the county. Detective W was driving and we responded out to that residence.

Upon arrival to the residence, we decided to watch the suspect's street for an hour or two. After about an hour, we observed an unrelated 25 year old white male come out of a residence and a vehicle was arriving at that unrelated house at the same moment. The white male appeared to be walking over toward our vehicle from a distance. Normally, the tint on our vehicles was dark enough that people could not see us inside the vehicle. However, the white male had instructed the arriving vehicle to turn around and shine the headlights through our front windshield.

As the other vehicle's headlights, started to shine on our windshield, I could only make out the dark outline of the white male as he walked closer. When the white male was about fifteen feet from our front bumper, I stated, "Oh, shit Detective W he's got a gun!" I had observed the outline of a handgun in the white male subject's right hand as he walked toward our vehicle. I jumped from the front passenger seat as I pulled my firearm and instructed the white male to put the gun down.

The white male still had the firearm at his side pointed toward the ground and looked like he knew that he had made a big mistake. The white male placed the handgun onto the ground and put both hands high into the air. Detective W and I approached and placed him into handcuffs.

We were able to determine that the white male did live at that address, he did not have a criminal history, and had a concealed weapons permit to carry a firearm. However, clearly the white male did not have the authority to approach a vehicle in the street with a firearm and the white male knew the gravity of his mistake. We could have charged the white male with improper exhibition of a firearm, but decided not to pursue any charges against him. We unloaded the white male's firearm and released him at the scene.

Chapter 27

Detective W and I went to an apartment building to locate a wanted suspect for possession of cocaine. The complex had an "L" shaped fenced parking lot that ran along the west and south side of the building. The building entry door required a code to enter. We had observed the suspect's vehicle parked in the lot and were sitting watching it.

As we waited, we happened to notice a vehicle in the parking lot that matched the color and model of one that was stolen during a recent residential burglary. I had Detective L drive onto the parking lot and check the vehicle tag to see if it was the stolen vehicle and he confirmed that it was stolen. We called the remainder of the unit to the area and now watched both the wanted suspect's vehicle and the stolen vehicle to see if anyone approached either of them. We ended up reading the residential burglary report that documented the stolen vehicle and learned that someone broke into the victim's residence, found keys, and took both of the victim's vehicles from the garage.

We scanned the rest of the parking lot and observed a possible match for the victim's second vehicle parked two spots away from the other stolen vehicle. We called for Detective L to drive back onto the parking lot to check the tag and he confirmed that we had also located the second stolen vehicle.

After a couple hours, a decision was made to have uniformed officers respond and simply recover the victim's two stolen vehicles. As the uniformed officers were pulling onto the parking lot, we observed a white male approach from the south and jump the fence to come onto the parking lot. We didn't have time to call off the uniformed officers. As soon as the white male saw the marked cruisers, he ran to the east and jumped over a six foot concrete wall that ran along the east side of the parking lot. I notified other units of what we had observed and initiated a foot pursuit after the white male to stop and detain him.

I climbed and started to jump over the six foot concrete wall and realized that the neighboring property had a six foot fence along its' property line a couple feet away. I continued and simply jumped over both by pushing off of the concrete wall with my left arm. The white male had crouched down in a hiding position on the north side of that section of the property, but ran to the east at the sight of me climbing the wall to come after him. I called to our units that the suspect had run to the east. I ran around the neighboring building and then eastbound in the same path that the suspect took, but he was nowhere in sight. I continued out to where the units were to the east and they advised that they never saw the white male suspect.

I realized immediately that I had injured my left shoulder as I had pushed off of the wall to clear the fence. I ended up having to go to the emergency room to document the injury and yes, I was prescribed the standard 800 milligrams Ibuprofen. I was pretty upset about the shoulder injury, because I had just recently started back to lifting weights at the gym. My elbow had taken about a year to heal well enough where I could lift weights again.

I continued working my regular shifts, but the shoulder did not seem like it was healing. I even attended about four weeks of physical therapy. I had an MRI and went to an orthopedic surgeon, who advised that I had torn the labrum in the shoulder. I continued working until the surgery, which was scheduled about two months after the injury. I certainly did not want to have another surgery, but the shoulder was painful to move and the surgeon advised that it would never heal on its' own.

I ended up having the shoulder surgery in April of 2012 and have basically not felt healthy since that surgery. I thought I knew what to expect, because I had previously had two right shoulder surgeries. About thirty hours after surgery, I started to have severe pain in my ribcage especially on my right side. At times the pain was so bad that I could hardly breathe, so I had to take shallow breaths during those moments. I decided not to go to the emergency room because I was scheduled to see the orthopedic surgeon on the fourth day after surgery.

I went to the surgeon and he simply advised that I must not have been supported enough on my right side during the surgery. The surgeon advised that there was no need to x-ray the ribcage because in his words, "It's not like you are going to have surgery on your ribs to correct anything." To this day, I have intermittent pains in my ribcage that have never been solved.

I started physical therapy for the shoulder and in hindsight, knew that things were very different with this recovery. During physical therapy, when I moved there was a tremor in my entire left arm and at times a violent tremor. The pain during the recovery was excruciating and I noticed that with any pain the tremor became accentuated. The pain was so bad in the shoulder that I could not even lay flat on my bed. I slept in a recliner at night for twelve weeks. The physical therapy lasted for fourteen weeks after the surgery and at the end of that, I simply told the surgeon to release me to return to work. I knew that I was going to take a long time to continue to recover.

During that time, I also continued going to appointments every three months with Dr. B, my neurologist. Dr. B could obviously see that the tremor in the arm had become worse. Dr. B also advised that tremor could increase with pain, so I hoped that was all that was happening. Dr. B explained that there was also several other types of medication that I could try to minimize the tremor, but I was always reluctant to try anything that would interfere with my reaction time or my job as a police officer.

As I returned to work, I knew that I was going to have to take it easy for a little while and baby the shoulder for recovery. I also found right away that I did not really want to be around too many people, because the tremor was now something that was out of my control. I almost never wanted to go to the police station, where I would run into many friends. I tried not to spend too much time with other officers on the street and was hoping that the tremor would decrease when the pain in the shoulder decreased. Other detectives in my unit knew about the tremor after my shoulder surgery and we even joked about it. There is almost nothing that police officers won't joke about, if given the chance.

The second week after I returned from my shoulder surgery, I was assigned to work the Republican National Convention. A few detectives from my unit were chosen to work the convention in an undercover capacity with FBI agents. The FBI agents were paired with each of us and each team was given a specific assignment. We were issued credentials and we met every day for briefings at the local FBI headquarters. I was assigned with Agent B and we had a pretty good week together. I laughed about the fact that nineteen years after graduating from college, I was finally working at the FBI.

After returning to work, I started noticing that my distance vision clarity was fluctuating. There were times that I could see normally and other times at the same distance things would be blurry. I would notice the differences when trying to read a vehicle tag or trying to identify a suspect that we would be looking at. There is a true art to being able to look at a prior picture of an individual and then positively identify a subject that you see in person as being the same individual. Even many police officers have difficulty with this task.

I had become very good at it, but my changing vision started to hinder that ability. I had prided myself in the past on having better distance vision than any officer sitting next to me. I wore contacts during college, but after college had the Lasik vision correction surgery and my results were incredible.

I went to an ophthalmologist for an appointment and was advised that there were not any problems with my eyes. The ophthalmologist told me that if the vision fluctuations continued that I needed to look for another medical cause, such as diabetes. I did follow up on that suggestion and checked my blood sugar for several weeks, but did not get any unusual readings.

I also started to notice that my thinking was changing and even simple things seemed to be challenging. The problems thinking and memory would fluctuate just like my vision, but not necessarily in unison with that problem. I really started to notice that my memory was not very good. I was forgetting street names, had to really think about the quickest routes to travel, and sometimes would forget what word I was trying to say. I worked in a unit with eighteen other people and there were times that I could not think of everyone's name even when I could see them. There were numerous weeks where I would take the time to envision where everyone's desk was located in the office and remind myself of each detective's name. These were my friends and this thinking was not normal. One time, I was returning to the office from dinner with Sergeant H in my truck and I missed the turn to our office that I had driven to for eight years. I simply played it off with a joke, but knew there was something else wrong.

I had been seeing Dr. B every three months for about eighteen months, so at my next appointment I talked to her about getting some type of brain scan. There was a little reluctance from Dr. B, because at that time, I don't believe she thought I had a serious problem. I was only

42 years old and many times I believe I was being compared to the many other patients in her office that were elderly. Dr. B ordered and set up a DAT-scan, which was a brand new type of scan specifically for Parkinson's disease. The scan utilized a radioactive drug to look at a specific area of the brain, view the activity, and record the level of dopamine produced. The test was so new that it took a couple of weeks to get the drug to complete the test.

***

I was still working my normal evening shift during all of this time period. Nobody knew that I had any serious problems, but me. We started working a commercial burglary pattern on midnights with both squads of the unit. The area of the pattern was so large that we all were covering separate businesses by ourselves. I was assigned at a gas station.

On about the third night, Detective C called over the radio, "Get some units to the 7-11 on Fourth Street, two black males just went into the front doors with masks and guns." It was about 0300 hours and I am sure that I wasn't the only detective that almost half asleep. I started my vehicle, threw it in gear and started to drive the twenty-five blocks to the 7-11. I confirmed over the radio the robbery location with Detective C, because there was a new 7-11 that had opened on a different street five blocks away. Many of our units were close to the store.

The suspects exited the store to the west and then ran around the rear to head eastbound. Detective C and Detective D were already on the parking lot of the store in their vehicles. As I started to drive eastbound on the avenue toward the store, I heard gunfire. Detective C advised that one of the suspects was down on the east side of the store and the other suspect continued east into a neighborhood. I drove past the front of the store, observed the suspect on the ground,

and continued eastbound to create an east perimeter. We had the second suspect contained and the suspect was located by a K-9 unit within a few minutes. I returned to the front of the 7-11 with all of the other detectives. Numerous uniformed officers had responded to assist and secured the scene. I definitely was not feeling like myself, so I simply tried to stay out of everyone else's way. I did not take any active responsibilities at the scene.

***

I had completed the DAT-scan and then on November 15, 2012 went to Dr. B's office for the results. Dr. B entered the room and simply stated, "Well, it came back positive, you have Parkinson's." After all of the changes that I had experienced over the last eighteen months, I was not surprised at all. I was confident that I would eventually be diagnosed with something and it ended up being Parkinson's disease.

I am sure that there was a certain routine that Dr. B's office used to break bad news like this to patients. Dr. B had the office social worker, Ms. E, on "stand-by" right outside the door. You never know how someone will react to tragic news. Ms. E came into the room with a handful of educational books and videos on Parkinson's and both of them stressed that the Parkinson's would "progress slowly over the next couple decades".

I remember my first thought was simply disappointment, because I really wanted to grow old. I wanted to work my full career to a retirement age in my late fifties, watch my daughter become independent in her life, and grow old with my wife. All of my grandparents lived to an average age of 83 years old and my parents and siblings were all still alive. I wanted to grow old, but that wasn't meant to be and sometimes that's just the way it is. I certainly knew firsthand that there are no guarantees in life.

I came home and told my wife and she was devastated. I had done such a good job at hiding so many of the changes that the diagnosis came as a complete shock to her even though she knew I had the scan completed. I remember after telling her the diagnosis, I told her that I was sorry, because I knew that I wasn't the only one affected by the diagnosis. Later that day, I told my 13 year old daughter about Parkinson's disease.

I simply went back to work. I had one more shift to work to finish out the week and then I was taking a week off for Thanksgiving. We had already made plans to travel up to Myrtle Beach, SC and have my parents stay with us in a beach condo. Any excitement about the trip had definitely been overshadowed by my Parkinson's diagnosis. I waited until we arrived at the beach condo and told my parents about the diagnosis.

I learned a great deal about Parkinson's disease and that research explained many of the symptoms and the changes that had occurred in my personality. Parkinson's disease is a chronic and progressive movement disorder, which means symptoms continue to worsen over time. The disease occurs when the substantia nigra region in the brain begins to die and the brain loses the ability to produce dopamine. The substantia nigra region controls both movement and emotions. Damage to this area of the brain can result in movement disorders, anxiety, sleep problems, and personality changes at a minimum. The cardinal symptoms of Parkinson's disease are tremor, slowness of movement, rigid muscles, and loss of balance or coordination.

I now knew what the problem was and had an explanation for my changes, but certainly didn't know what my future would be.

Chapter 28

I always arrived at least fifteen minutes early to work. I always liked to ensure that I had all of my equipment in order and wanted to know what the plan was for the day, prior to really getting started. After my Thanksgiving week vacation, I arrived at work early like any other shift. Initially, I was in the office by myself, but then Detective P and Sergeant H arrived. I had no intention of trying to keep my problem a secret any longer and assumed maybe I had not been as successful at hiding it as maybe I thought anyway. I walked into Sergeant H's office behind him and simply told him that I had been diagnosed with Parkinson's disease. I think the news of my diagnosis hit him harder than it had even hit me, because he was not expecting it. Sergeant H was a great sergeant and a good man and he made it clear that I could ask for anything that I needed.

When the remainder of my squad arrived at work, I simply told everyone about the diagnosis. Several of my friends asked numerous questions, but I really didn't have all the answers. I simply planned to work as long as I could and keep myself as healthy as I could. Unfortunately the rest was out of my control.

I started researching the best supplements that I could start taking as well as all of the theories behind Parkinson's disease. The saddest fact that I learned was that the best medicine available for Parkinson's was L-dopa, under the prescription name Sinemet. L-dopa was discovered and used in the late 1960's for Parkinson's and almost fifty years later was still the best medicine. The only progress that had been made was improvements in how the medication was absorbed by the body, which made the medicine more effective.

Unfortunately for me, my symptoms and the negative impact of Parkinson's disease progressed at a much quicker pace than anyone expected. The initial Parkinson's medication did not have any effect, so I switched within a month and started taking two other medications. I am not certain how effective they were either. It is hard to know if any medication is helping when you continue to get worse. I also attempted to go to a homeopath in a different city. I tried several "remedies" suggested by the homeopath, but none of them had any impact on my symptoms.

Within six months of my diagnosis of Parkinson's disease, my Parkinson's symptoms were significantly worse. The tremor had started to progress into my left leg, which was expected, just not expected so quickly. I had headaches that originally started behind my eyes and then later progressed to pinpoint headaches that would start and stop quickly at various spots in my head. I was also still having the vision fluctuations, some confusion and memory problems, and I would become extremely lethargic. I had problems swallowing food at times without also drinking liquids and trouble with even speaking. I felt like I was thinking and moving in slow motion and that I had aged significantly. At times I had lost my fine motor skills and some of my smooth muscle movements, which made me, feel clumsy. Physical tasks, stress, and even using my mind to think too much seemed to cause the tremor to become worse. I lost some of my facial expression and there were moments that I found it hard to physically make a smile. This symptom is known as the "Parkinson's mask" and I could actually feel that I had lost the ability to move my facial muscles. All of the symptoms would come and go at varying intensities, like waves in the ocean.

I felt like I was fading so fast that I made changes in my personal life. I sold my two story house and moved into a maintenance free villa with the master bedroom on the first floor. I felt like I already had to make plans for the worse-case scenario. The Sergeant B that was killed in the line of duty told me one time that a good friend will help you move, but a great friend will help you move a body. Luckily, I was able to get my good friends from work to come and help my family move.

During all of these problems, I was still working my normal evening shifts trying to keep up. The sheer exhaustion that I would feel sometimes was too overwhelming and I could do nothing but take a nap. At various times during the day, it would feel like my brain needed to shut off and sleep. Many nights, I simply rode by myself on the street, because at some point during every shift I would have to sleep for a quick nap. I almost found sleep to work better than any medication. There were numerous times that our squad had to change shifts and this also made things much worse for me.

***

We started working two adult black male suspects that were committing daytime burglaries. Our unit had previously arrested both of them on a prior daytime pattern, so working them again was going to be a challenge. We had generated enough evidence against the two that a judge issued a warrant to place a GPS unit on the main suspect's vehicle. The device made following the suspects a little easier, but we still had to witness them committing the crimes.

After working them for a couple days, the two suspects started driving around very early on the third day. All of our detectives had not even made it into work, when the suspects started on the move. The suspects drove out of our City and into a county that was to the south of ours. The suspects made a quick stop at a Home Depot and we later learned that this was to purchase additional burglary tools. The suspects drove to a residential neighborhood and located a residence that they liked. Some of our detectives were able to arrive on location and start calling the actions of the suspects.

Detective W and I were riding together and were still in route when other detectives advised that the suspects were committing the residential burglary. Part of our difficulty was the distance they traveled and the rest was not being familiar with that county. The suspects were being handcuffed as Detective W and I pulled up to the victim's residence. I was able to contribute a little to the case, because I found the receipt from Home Depot that the suspect had thrown next to the bushes. The receipt showed that the suspect purchased a brand new crow bar for the day's activities.

***

We worked another commercial burglary pattern on a black male suspect that was possibly breaking into businesses in several different cities. There was enough evidence to also obtain a warrant to place a GPS tracker on that suspect's vehicle. The black male suspect was using his girlfriend's gray Buick to commit the burglaries. The first night that we worked the suspect we were still on evening shift and we were able to get the tracker onto the suspect's vehicle. We all checked off work at 0200 hours and went home.

Detective S obtained a notice from the GPS that the suspect's vehicle was moving at approximately 0230 hours. Detective S called Sergeant H and asked if we should all come back into work. At the time, the department was really monitoring overtime, so Sergeant H advised him that we would have to start working the pattern the following night. Unfortunately, the suspect did go out and commit a commercial burglary in another city, but there was no other evidence linking the suspect to the crime. We simply knew that the suspect's vehicle was close to the commercial burglary that occurred.

The next night we all started working the midnight shift for that commercial burglary pattern. We worked the pattern for eleven nights straight and the suspect never left his apartment. We stopped working the pattern and moved on to something else, because the suspect was no longer active. A couple weeks later we went to a restaurant for dinner and the black female cashier looked familiar. As we left the restaurant, I observed the black female's gray Buick in the parking lot, which was the suspect's vehicle. It sure is a small world.

***

We were contacted by the Homicide unit when we came in for our evening shift. Earlier that day, an 18 year old black male suspect had shot and killed another 18 year old black male. The Homicide Unit had researched the suspect and believed that they knew the location where he was hiding.

We responded to the location, which was in a residential neighborhood and the suspect was believed to be hiding inside a single story residence. The residence was located in the middle of the block on the south side of the avenue and had an open carport on the east side of it.

Once the sun had gone down, it became difficult to watch the residence, but the activity there did increase. There were several subjects going in and out of the residence. We had K-9 Officer P near the location for a take down once we observed the suspect. Eventually, we observed the suspect come out the front door with a young black female and walk under the carport. I called for K-9 Officer P to approach from the west along the front yards and other officers to be ready to move in behind K-9 Officer P. I approached along the front yards from the east. K-9 Officer P and I arrived at the residence at the same time and we challenged the suspect as he stood beneath the carport in the dark.

The suspect was cooperative and was handcuffed without incident. I walked him to a marked police cruiser that arrived on scene and the suspect told me that he wanted to tell a detective his side of the story. The suspect was later interviewed by homicide detectives.

K-9 Officer P was a good friend and attempted to help me with some advice for Parkinson's disease not long after my diagnosis. K-9 Officer P explained that his mother-in-law had recently passed away and she had Parkinson's disease. He explained that she had a doctor in another city that administered glutathione injections, which were the only treatment that helped her. I followed up on K-9 Officer P's advice and did find a doctor to try the glutathione injections, but did not receive any improvement from them.

***

I had to make the decision to transfer to dayshift. Our dayshift seemed to usually work set hours as opposed to the evening shift that kept having to change its' schedule. I also hoped that working earlier in the day would help prevent me from becoming so exhausted. I had an incident that triggered my decision, when I drove home one evening.

I lived about thirty miles from work. During my last few months on evening shift, I always had to stop and take a quick nap on my way home, because I became too tired to drive straight home. We usually checked off work at 0200 hours and I would normally make it home around 0300 hours. We checked off work at the usual time of 0200 hours and I was driving home. The next thing I remember was "waking up" at 0330 hours and I was still driving around, but I was in another city. I had to drive to look at a street sign to even know where I was at. I learned that if I became too tired, I didn't know what to expect. A couple of weeks later, I was able to transfer to dayshift.

The one positive thing about changing to dayshift was I was going to have Detective L as my partner again and I was going to be working with Detective C, one of my original partners in the unit. I quickly found that things were different on the job, and it became so hard to function that I could barely make it through the day. My cognitive abilities to think and to do two things at once were disappearing at times. My muscles would become so stiff sitting in the vehicle that I found it hard to move right away, when I stepped out of the car. I still pushed myself and did the job, because I was not ready to leave. Sometimes, I believe I operated on auto-pilot when making some arrests.

I am pretty certain everyone else saw my physical and emotional decline. I had to attend the annual mobile field force, or "riot", training and I ran into one of my old sergeants, who had been promoted to Lieutenant. Lieutenant S came up to me and asked, "Hey Mike is everything alright with you, you seem so serious?" I told Lieutenant S that I had Parkinson's disease and he didn't initially believe me. I think he thought that I was telling a bad joke. In the past, I was always joking around about everything and would sometimes be the funniest guy in the room. That had all changed, not because I was now sad that I had Parkinson's, but because the part of my brain that controlled human emotion was dying and even my own personality was now different.

Since I was working dayshift, I would tend to run into so many more friends, because the majority of employees at the police department worked dayshift. I was still reluctant to make frequent trips to the station, because things were so different for me. My Lieutenant was Lieutenant M and he finally advised me on his own not to go to the station anymore. I know he was trying to help me stay on the job as long as I could make it and he was a tremendous help. The news of my diagnosis had slowly been making its' way through the department anyway. Everyone knows bad news travels fast. A few times, I ran into friends that had not seen me in a while or heard my news and they always looked surprised when they saw me. Over the last couple years, I had lost about 20 pounds and all of my muscle mass, so my physical appearance was different too.

On one dayshift, I ran into (retired) Major R. I had worked with Major R through negotiating the police contract with the City for 15 years. I had just recently reluctantly removed myself from the union negotiating team for the police department. At the time, I knew I couldn't allow the department's administration or any of the City attorneys to learn how sick I was. Major R ended up telling me about Atlas Orthogonal adjustments in chiropractic medicine and took the time to meet with me later at his chiropractor's office. I ended up seeing Major R's chiropractor and having that adjustment to see if that changed anything for me.

I was still going to the Movement Disorder Center every three months. Sometimes I would see Dr. B and other times I would see Physician Assistant T. I was definitely satisfied with their professionalism and competence, but there were certain symptoms that I would discuss with both of them that they would always tell me were not very common in early Parkinson's disease. Those symptoms were the vision changes, confusion and memory problems, problems swallowing, ringing in my ears, and I still had intermittent pains in my ribcage and abdomen. Physician Assistant T had already tried increasing the dosage of my medication and my symptoms continued to progress. I even reviewed my brain scan with them and could easily see the damage to my brain that appeared different on the scan.

I decided that I was going to go to the Mayo Clinic to ensure there wasn't also something else wrong or something else that could be done for me. I knew that if something didn't change, I was going to have to leave the police department. I obviously, also had concerns for the future of my health after I would have to retire. I had learned that there were several types of atypical parkinsonism-syndromes that were commonly mistaken for Parkinson's disease and they progress quickly like "Parkinson's on steroids". I won't bore you with the details, so we'll just say it's a short story.

It took a couple of months to get to my initial appointment at the Mayo Clinic and then I had about eight full days of appointments spread over the following month for various medical tests.

***

In between my trips to the Mayo Clinic, I still worked my dayshift on the street with Detective L. By this time, we decided between the two of us that Detective L would do all of the driving on-duty. In one of our discussions, Detective L told me that he loved being my partner and even if I was simply a ride-along he would happy with that. A ride-along was a term that referred to a civilian that rode with a police officer to see what an officer does on the job. Over my career, I had accommodated many ride-along individuals, including children from the Make-A-Wish Foundation. At one time, I was a strong leader in our unit and as a uniformed officer and I was well respected throughout the entire police department, and I was now on my way to becoming a ride-along.

***

Our unit was actively looking for a maroon Honda Accord that was driven by a known black female suspect that was wanted for two bank robberies. We knew the suspect's home address, but she was out driving around. We wanted to locate her quickly and prevent another bank robbery. Detective L was joking around and stated, "Where would I go if I were a bank robber with a lot of cash. Probably to that Save-a-lot and buy a bunch of meat." I looked over to the Save-a-lot and observed what I thought was the suspect's vehicle. We turned our vehicle around and returned to

259

find the suspect's vehicle parked right in front of the entry doors.

The suspect walked outside after a couple minutes with a cart full of groceries, including meat. The suspect was arrested without any further incident.

***

During my last few months, I was still very active on the street. The department had recently equipped three vehicles with a GPS device that could be fired at and stick to a vehicle that refused to stop. Detective L's vehicle became one of those vehicles and we used the device on a couple violent felons, a burglary suspect, and a stolen vehicle. All those incidents resulted in arrests of numerous suspects. We located a suspect vehicle right after a residential burglary, had a short pursuit, and arrested two black males after a short foot chase. I dislocated my ring finger on my left hand during that incident. On another case, we caught two suspects that ran on foot from a stolen vehicle. I broke the tip of my right pinky finger punching the suspect a couple times in his side, because he wanted to physically resist during the arrest. I simply kept going to work and doing what I could, because I knew my days were numbered.

***

Just prior to one of my trips to the Mayo Clinic, Detective L and I went out into the county to check for a suspect at an apartment complex. We drove through the apartment complex and did not see our suspect's vehicle. As we were leaving, we observed a white Nissan Murano parked in the parking lot and there was one of those that had been recently stolen in our City. The stolen vehicle was owned by a local rental car company and the officer that took the report could not initially get the tag number, so the tag was not known at the time. I wrote down the tag number of the vehicle in the parking lot and was going to research it.

We left the complex and a few minutes later, I discovered that the tag on the vehicle was registered to the same rental car company linked to a different vehicle. As we returned to the apartment complex to see if the vehicle was still there, I called the rental car company. I was able to speak with a manager and obtain the vehicle identification number (VIN) of the stolen Murano. The vehicle was still in the parking lot and the VIN matched. We called the rest of our unit to our location, conducted further research, and located the apartment number of the known suspect listed in the original auto theft report.

Detective L and I set up on the east side of the complex and the vehicle was parked on the west side. When the suspect came out of his apartment, I exited our vehicle and followed him as he went westbound through the complex toward the stolen vehicle. Other detectives and uniformed deputies from the county were in place to take down the suspect at the vehicle.

During the takedown the suspect was able to run eastbound on foot. I was standing in between two of the apartment buildings and the suspect rounded the corner running right toward me. I drew my issued firearm and yelled, "Police officer, get on the ground!" Without hesitation the suspect stopped in his tracks and lay on his stomach, as other officers rounded the same corner and handcuffed him. I was concerned, because during the take-down the muscles across my upper back felt like they were in a knot and my movements became restricted. I did not know it at the time, but this would be my last take-down with my firearm.

***

I came back from my final Mayo Clinic appointment totally defeated and I had run out of options. The bottom line was that I had Parkinson's disease and there was basically nothing else that doctors could do

261

for me. There was only one unusual reading that the Mayo Clinic doctors noted and that was a "weakly positive" ANA blood test. The doctors suggested that I retake the ANA blood test within six months. This test reads the antinuclear antibodies in the blood and predicts autoimmune diseases.

As far as learning if I had the "Parkinson's on steroids", I was advised, that question could not be answered until an autopsy is performed. The head neurologist suggested that I change my medication to the best medicine for Parkinson's, which was Sinemet (L-dopa).

I never worked another day on the street as a police officer and I was granted a disability retirement two months later.

Chapter 29

The time period between my actual Parkinson's diagnosis and my disability hearing was about 18 months. After hearing the initial diagnosis and the fact that Parkinson's disease progresses over decades, I had maybe foolishly thought that I could have finished my career but that wasn't meant to be.

I left the police department where I worked for just over 16 years and all of that time had passed in a flash. I was not celebrating anything, so there wasn't any retirement party or big send off. I owe a big debt of gratitude to Detective C who helped me finalize everything at the department. Detective C worked with Lieutenant M to obtain my retired police identification and a very nice plaque issued by the department with all of my badges displayed. I received five cards in the mail that I was very pleased to get and then I was gone.

***

Good police officers talk about and look forward to an early retirement compared to the rest of the world, but when the time comes time for leaving you have to carry them out of the police station kicking and screaming. From the very first hour that a sworn police officer works on the street, they have a contract with the pension plan that they work under. My contract, or plan description, stated that I had to work a minimum of 25 years and I would earn 3% of my final pay for each of those years. This meant that after working 25 years my pension payment would have been 75% of my final pay. To receive those benefits of the contract, every sworn officer was required to contribute 7% of their current pay toward the pension plan. Pension plans themselves are created to reward long and loyal service.

There was a "safety net" within that same contract for any police officer that was not able to finish a 25 year career. An officer that was disabled due to health problems (non-service connected), was retired and collected their accrued amount or 25% of pay minimum. An officer that was disabled due to a service related incident (service connected), was retired and collected their accrued amount or a minimum of 60% of pay minimum.

The doctors that treat Parkinson's patients do not necessarily look for the definitive cause of the Parkinson's disease that responsibility is left to researchers. Dr. B initially acknowledged numerous head injuries in my past history, but simply treated me for all of my Parkinson's symptoms. All of the different doctors at the Mayo Clinic, both verbally and in several written reports, simply noted the head injuries as being a factor in the Parkinson's disease. Since I had five documented head injuries as a police officer, I was certain that they contributed to the early Parkinson's disease diagnosis. The average age for being diagnosed with Parkinson's disease is around 62 years of age. I filed for the service related disability.

Initially, the City's police pension board approved a non-service connected disability and stated I would have to prove my case for the service connected disability in a full pension hearing. Unfortunately for me, I was on my own. Since my first day on the job, I had paid my union dues to the police union and paid 7% of my pay to the pension plan, but neither of those entities provided any assistance toward proving my disability case. I had trouble maintaining concentration, problems with memory, numerous physical problems, and I had to fight this battle on my own. I do owe a huge thank you to my friend Mrs. W for keeping things on track at the pension office. I spent hundreds of hours creating an argument for my case and then simply read it to the pension board.

Part of my case was simply educating the pension board on Parkinson's disease. In my research, I discovered that there are four known theories for the cause of Parkinson's disease and they are 1) a unique genetic mutation, 2) exposure to environmental toxins, 3) injecting yourself with a specific synthetic narcotic, and 4) head injuries. In my case, the theory of head injuries was the only theory that fit.

In 2009, the State of Indiana changed their laws for all emergency personnel to make a Parkinson's disease diagnosis automatically presumed to be a service connected disability. In January of 2014, the Federal Department of Veteran's Affairs changed its' disability rules for anyone with head trauma to make Parkinson's disease automatically covered as a service connected disability for the 1.4 million active and the 2.3 million retired military personnel. In July of 2014, the NFL settled a class action lawsuit by establishing a trust of over $765 million to cover over 20,000 former players and make diseases caused from head injuries automatically covered through that trust. All of these changes were made because recent scientific research showed that head injuries were linked to Parkinson's disease.

I recognized that my disability case was unique for the pension board, because they were used to reviewing cases involving identifiable injuries that were linked to one specific trauma. I also realized that the pension board needed to ensure that they did not approve any fraudulent claims and protect the City's interest in the pension plan. I pointed out to the pension board that they also had a responsibility to use their discretionary authority to make fair decisions for each and every officer in the plan. Police officers rely on the "safety net" of the pension plan when taking risks on the street in the performance of their duties.

I set up a conference phone call with Dr. B and gave the pension board an opportunity to question her directly about my case. Dr. B advised the pension board that based on my age the head injuries would be considered the primary cause of the Parkinson's disease. The pension board had numerous other questions for Dr. B, but they ultimately made a decision to unanimously approve my service connected disability. I would not have been successful without the testimony from Dr. B. There was no celebration, because I still walked out of the pension hearing with Parkinson's disease.

***

The next month, I completed another ANA blood test as recommended by the Mayo Clinic and the results came back this time as positive. I was advised to make an appointment with a rheumatologist. The rheumatologist was Dr. S and she wanted to run many other blood tests. When those tests came back, the ANA blood test was even higher and I started to have additional symptoms such as increased joint and muscle pains, kidney pains, and skin problems. The arthritic pains were worse in my hands, feet, and my lower back. At times, my hands hurt so bad I could barely take the top off of my prescription medication or simply take things out of my pockets. There were times that my confusion would start and I literally had to remind myself where I was at or where I was traveling to. Other times it would feel like someone flipped a reset button on my brain and still other moments I would be stuck in a "fog" staring into the distance. I firmly believe that there is only one thing worse than losing your mind, and that is to know that you are losing your mind.

Dr. S advised that she wanted to test everything again in three months, so I continued to wait for help. I spoke with Dr. B, my neurologist and she advised that the positive ANA reading did not have anything to do with Parkinson's disease, and it would almost be impossible to separate out Parkinson's symptoms and autoimmune symptoms into categories.

Dr. S received the same increased results three months later and I still had all the new symptoms and some of the old ones getting worse. I had been seeing Dr. S for six months and waiting for some additional help from her. I will never forget the words spoken to me by Dr. S, as she stated, "I am not prepared to offer any treatment at this time." I wasn't going to argue with her or try to convince her to help me, so I simply left her office. I will have to say that I was a little aggravated that it took her six months to tell me that she was not going to help me.

During that six month time period of waiting, I had continued to research Parkinson's disease and numerous medical problems on my own. The positive reading on the ANA blood test and several of my symptoms were related to autoimmune diseases. I found that there seemed to be one common theory within all autoimmune diseases and that was that they were caused by parasites. I researched further to find the best type of treatment for parasites and I came to diatomaceous earth.

Now, I was actually familiar with diatomaceous earth, because I had used it in my swimming pool filters for the last 18 years. During all that time, I never considered eating the damn stuff. Diatomaceous earth is fossilized remains of hard shelled algae that lived millions of years ago, it is considered a sedimentary rock, and is about 89% silica. The "food grade" diatomaceous earth is used as a "mechanical" insecticide, because it is not a poison. The microscopic diatoms are extremely hard and the sharp edges will kill any pests, including parasites, but they are hardly even abrasive to a human.

The testimonials on the internet were almost unbelievable, and I am well aware that you can't believe everything you read on the internet. Throughout everything, I had never had any stomach problems, which would be a common symptom from parasites. I had always had an iron gut, so I really did not know what to expect from taking the diatomaceous earth, but I was willing try it, like I tried so many other things.

I started taking the diatomaceous earth or what I call "dirt" and within a week I realized that I was starting to feel better. The arthritic feelings in my hands and feet and other joints had started to decrease. My mind started to feel like it could work again. Since the "dirt" seemed like it was helping me, I researched further. I learned that there were diet suggestions on things to eat and things to avoid when dealing with parasites and I built my diet around them. Within a month, I felt like 95% of all the arthritis and muscle pains were gone, which meant I could move around easier. The biggest change is the fact that I feel like I have much of my mind back, and I started writing this book two months ago to prove it.

Today, when I start to talk about parasites, I still feel like I am talking to people about Martians. I will have to say that I would be skeptical if I had not had this experience myself. Before my experience, I always assumed that a parasite was something that you ingested when drinking dirty water in a third world country. There are over a thousand different types of parasites that can infect the human body. I was shocked to learn that just one parasite in particular has infected at least 23% of Americans and 85% of Western Europeans. How has this been kept a secret?

I never scientifically proved that I had (or have) any type of parasite, nor do I feel the need to do so. I simply took a supplement that is known to kill parasites and many of my symptoms improved. I am just happy that I have had the improvement and that I can think more clearly.

Strangely it seems embarrassing to talk about a parasite that you might have had (or have). Americans will tell strangers about a bronchitis infection, but would never speak of parasites. I would probably keep it a secret too, but I believe there are millions of other people in the world with various ailments that would want to know this information to research it for themselves. I find it a little unusual that Americans will treat all our pets and livestock for parasites and assume that parasites know to leave us humans alone.

Unfortunately, this was not the miracle cure for everything or the cure for Parkinson's disease and maybe that is coming soon. I still have a tremor on the entire left side of my body as well as the other Parkinson's symptoms. I am certain that the damage that I viewed on my brain scan didn't simply disappear. I accept the fact that things will change for me again and that is just the way it is, because in this world people get sick and it's not always someone else. No matter what happens in the next chapter, I still have the rest of my life in front of me.

Well, that is my story. So what have I learned through my life and what lesson do I get to take away from it. I definitely learned one thing you should never trust giving the camera to the guy with Parkinson's disease.

I certainly enjoyed my police career and I miss the brotherhood that I had to leave behind. I know in my heart that I worked as long as I could have and maybe a little longer. I would definitely come back for more, if I could. I saw a great deal of tragedy along the way and there are memories that can't be erased. I can only hope that the things that I did in my career helped prevent some tragedies and helped my fellow officers.

Just like my first day in the police academy, life is full of learning opportunities. You can normally learn something from every person you ever have contact with in life. I have had numerous people come in and out of my life along the way that I have helped or who have helped me. I know as an officer there were countless times that I had to strike suspects, but for every strike that I took in my career there were ten times as many people that I was able to help in some way. I know on the opposite side of every arrest are known victims and their families, not to mention preventing future victims. My advice to all of the sheepdogs in the world, with policing in your DNA, is to keep fighting the good fight and I thank you for your service.

There is one thing that I never mentioned in my book and that is my faith of the presence of God in my life that was always with me through all my trials. I am not one to preach too much to others, but believe that I have a strong moral foundation that directs me to always do what is right and my faith gives me a unique perspective on life. I know that bad things happen to people and that there is evil in this world and I accept that is the way it is. I know that some people are given one day in life and others are given 100 years. My faith tells me that my main goal in life is to get my family and me into heaven. As strange as it may sound to some, I know that God led me to the diatomaceous earth for help and I hope somehow I can share that with others through my story. There have been many people through time that have stated in one way or another that "We don't know what we don't know" and that is true in every aspect of life, including medicine.

About six months after I had taken a disability retirement from my career, I was returning from dinner with a group of four other people. I could hear the conversation from the back seat discussing the suicide of a famous actor, who had recently been diagnosed with Parkinson's disease. A comment was made, "It Can't Be That Bad". I saw that comment as the connection between my police career and my Parkinson's disease.

Any person standing on the outside and looking in simply can't have the ability to empathize, to understand, or have the perspective, as someone on the inside does. Unfortunately, I know firsthand the hidden issues of a disability involving the brain. I know how the person you once were no longer exists and how there becomes a "new normal" in your life. The design cover for my book came easy to me, because I have always thought of Parkinson's as a lonely disease. No one understands Parkinson's, not doctors, not your friends, not your family, and not even the Parkinson's patient. The disease is there and the symptoms are all around you like the waves on the ocean. No matter how much help you have with Parkinson's, it is still your own challenge and one that must be fought by you.

It is a true statement, that in the future I don't know 100% where I will be in life or what I will be doing, and there is only one thing that I know for certain, neither do you.